JOY IN THE VALLEY

THE MOUNTAIN IS MY BENCHMARK
— *Sophia Melanie Manning*

JOY IN THE VALLEY

A self-improvement narrative for abundance and enrichment in daily life

Copyright © 2008 by Sophia Melanie Manning
All rights reserved

Printed in the United States of America
All rights reserved. This book, or parts thereof, may not be reproduced in any form without permission.

The Paradoxical Commandments are reprinted by permission of the author. (c) Copyright Kent M. Keith 1968, renewed 2001.

Scriptures are taken from the HOLY BIBLE, King James Version, New International Version and New American Standard Bible.

Quotes from known and unknown writers are accredited to individuals according to the sources of reference.

Cover photo by *Jerry Brown*

Self-published by *Sophia Melanie Manning*
A product of Entertainment Now Network, Inc.

ISBN – 978-0-615-25496-8
Library of Congress Cataloging-in-Publication Data

BLESSINGS AND PRAISES TO SOPHIA MANNING AND JOY IN THE VALLEY

Sophia, you are on the right track and you have **all my blessings**. Your book reveals your knowledge of life weaved together with your personal experiences and with great passion for your audiences all together driven by your faith in God. This is an inspirational piece of work! **Father Zachaeues Kirangu, PhD – Priest, Our Lady of The Assumption**

I read Sophia's book during a time I was going through my own valley. Her personal experience together with the powerful quotes and the everyday practical insight on overcoming life's teachings gave me strength and inspired me to continue walking through the valley with great joy! Sophia's book is not simply another book with general indications for personal growth, it is a book like no other that will make you feel someone is holding your hand as you fulfill your life's purpose. Thank you Sophia for your valuable contribution!
May the Universe conspire to make this book a bestseller for you are a blessing to humanity and deserve it all!
All my love and blessings to you my dear friend!
Cristina Oliva-Klos; Founder & Managing Director
HB International - A School for One World

This is a book that needs to be read. It offers great insight on life and the spiritual help in one's life. Too often we do not take the time to reflect on ourselves and what has taken us to the journey thru life. Sophia has made this very informative and interesting; you won't be disappointed in any way. – **Albert Rayl, Author, Beyond My Wildest Dreams; Beyond My Wildest Dreams, becoming a "Big Game Hunter"; B to B Candle Making, Beginners to Business; Rayl Family Cookbook**

Joy In The Valley is "heart-wrenching, soul-stirring and simply engulfing" - want to be inspired or motivated? Read the book! Sophia has raised the bar significantly by communicating the true meaning of "joy" as it relates to everyday life and her writing style has truly intrigued me. - **Errol Anthony Wilkes, Actor/film maker**

Table of Contents

INTRODUCTION 7
FORWARD 11
CHAPTER 1 17
   DISCOVERY 17
CHAPTER 2 29
   JOURNEY THROUGH THE VALLEY 29
CHAPTER 3 41
   IN THE VALLEY 41
CHAPTER 4 59
   TESTING IN THE VALLEY 59
CHAPTER 5 85
   FACING THE VALLEY 85
CHAPTER 6 107
   JOY IN THE VALLEY 107
CHAPTER 7 119
   RECOVERY 119
   ABOUT THE AUTHOR 146

"Thanks and praises to the Creator of the Universe who is and always will be The Father of Creation – Your kingdom of Love is in my heart" – Your daughter Sophia

RYANNE-SEYMOUR, THE SACRIFICES I MADE FOR YOU, BROUGHT ME JOY IN THE VALLEY – Mother's Love

Then a woman said, speak to us of Joy and Sorrow.

And he answered:

Your joy is your sorrow unmasked. And the selfsame well from which your laughter rises was oftentimes filled with your tears. And how else can it be? The deeper that sorrow carves into your being, the more joy you can contain. Is not the cup that holds your wine the very cup that was burned in the potter's oven? And is not the lute that soothes your spirit, the very wood that was hallowed with knives?

When you are joyous, look deep into your heart and you shall find it is only that which has given you sorrow that is giving you joy. When you are sorrowful look again in your heart, and you shall see that in truth you are weeping for that which has been your delight – Kahlil Gibran – The Prophet 1923

INTRODUCTION

JOY IN THE VALLEY

DISCOVERY TO RECOVERY

"Joy in the midst of long-suffering" would perhaps be another good way to entitle this story. Literally, that is the basis of this book; *"double for trouble"* could also be a subtitle as both joy and long-suffering are fruits of the spirit. As I encountered a time of testing and unpleasant situations which I refer to as the valley season, without always being aware, I experienced joy in an unspeakable way and in essence, both joy and long suffering were working for my good simultaneously.

This story refers to state-of-being, circumstances, situations, the significant healthy fruit that was cultivated – *"Joy"* as a result of *"long suffering",* the fertilizer that balanced the fruit. Negative seeds were planted by adversaries and as I became aware, I chose love to combat the devices used against me which resulted in redemption and complete deliverance. "Long-suffering", a fruit of the Spirit; though unpleasant, is that which fertilizes the soul and spirit and brings abundant life. If we are consciously aware of the substance it produces, we will admit that fertilizer is nourishing to growth and the nutrients it provides hinder malnutrition. I can say from experience that fertilizer and adversity are somewhat similar as I grew up amongst live-stock and agricultural farmers. I had first- hand experience with growth periods of various crops, trees, and animals and I remember the nutrients that fertilizer provided for crops and animals as they grew, and also the unpleasant smell that it carried; I therefore used this thought to encourage myself and to keep the negative voices including guilt and condemnation from being entertained in my spirit.

As I experienced the valley season, I chose to take an optimistic view and like platinum, the results are refined into valuable long-lasting materials. Simply put, while experiencing a series of challenging situations, one-after-the other in a lengthy season, I was faced with the choices of waddling into self-pity, lowering my self-worth by retaliating, seek revenge or refuge from other human beings, or face it with love, be productive, add to myself worth and to the lives of others who encounter similar situations. With tenacity and resilience, I chose to be productive, improve my quality of life and practice loving the agents of adversity as I learned that they too have purpose and may just be the bridge that God uses to bring me His promises. I have realized during the times of testing that it sometimes take interacting with opposing forces that one is enlightened.

Og Mandino, a pioneer and one of my favorite authors once wrote *"obstacles are necessary for success because in all careers of importance, victory comes only after many struggles and countless defeats. Yet each struggle, each defeat, sharpens your skills and strengths, your courage and your endurance, your ability and your confidence and thus each obstacle is a comrade-in-arms forcing you to become better ...*

or quit. Each rebuff is an opportunity to move forward; turn away from them, avoid them, and you throw away your future".

This excerpt was like the highest dosage of medicine that contributed to the growth of my character and personhood, during times when fierce situations came against me, "they did not prevail". With God's grace and humble-pride, I boldly declare that God has made me like the cedar in Lebanon and I must be confident and encourage myself as I found that in the valley, people of like temperament were rather scarce. Booker T. Washington said in his days of adversity that *'Character, not circumstances, makes the man. I will permit no man to narrow or degrade my soul by making me hate him."*

The purpose of this book is to remind myself and others that there are hidden treasures in us and it sometimes take seasons of such for God to reveal the true person in us. *"He made darkness his secret place" – [Psalm 18 v. 11].* It brings great joy for me to share the story itself, the way I handled it, how it handled me, the seeds I sowed and the many benefits I reaped. As I share my story with transparency, I hope it will bring joy to someone's valley, with love and the notion to enrich, encourage, enhance, develop strength, add value and improve lives, as challenges present themselves. I think it is safe to say that it is the inner being that brings true inspiration which results in one's destined aspiration which is what is conveyed in this book.

This story is dedicated to my fellow human kind from every walk of life that experience a valley season. I would like to encourage you with these words from Rev. S. Chadwick, *"The desperate days are the stepping-stones in the path of light. They seem to have been God's opportunity and man's school of wisdom. Desperation is better than despair."* I echo this as an expert witness and with boldness declare that *joy* is in the valley.

FORWARD

The purpose of the valley season is the experience and wisdom I gained, the defining and refining moments and the results that were proven at the end of the "long-suffering". I have discovered that in a quest for self-improvement and self-awareness, it is perhaps better to ask questions, rather than receive answers as questions brings intrigue and conviction, thus the essence of the soul and spirit of a man can find reason for growth and improvement.

LORD MAKE ME AN INSTRUMENT OF THY PEACE

Where there is hatred, let me sow love;
Where there is injury, pardon;
Where there is doubt, faith;
Where there is despair, hope;
Where there is darkness, light;
Where there is sadness; joy
O divine Master, grant that I may not so much seek
To be consoled as to console;
To be understood as to understand;
To be loved as to love
For it is in giving that we receive;
It is in pardoning that we are pardoned;
It is in dying to self that we are born to eternal life –
St. Francis of Assisi

The prayer of St. Francis of Assisi caught my attention on a very cold damp day in the winter of 1996 in England. While seated in the lobby of a bank waiting for my cousin to finish work so we could have dinner at her favorite seafood restaurant, the picture on the cover of a magazine had the most fascinated abstract painting that literally blew my mind. By nature I am a *surrealist*, I absolutely cherish the arts and am intrigued by *"weird looking stuff" - paintings, fashion and styles.* Of course, I picked up the magazine and as I opened it, the words "LORD LET ME BE AN INSTRUMENT OF THY PEACE" were written in the boldest print on the page. I read the prayer and was touched to the degree that I walked over to the receptionist and asked for paper to write on. I hastily wrote the prayer and placed it in a compartment in my purse.

While seated in the restaurant waiting to be served, I pulled the prayer out and read it several times before I was served. When I got to the flat where I was lodging, I typed the prayer in an email and sent it to myself. I meditated on the words as it had such meaning to me, and while at the time, I was enjoying life; living, loving and learning, something about that prayer struck me, I just couldn't put my hand on where in my life to apply it; there was just a connection.

Romans 8:26 – *We know not what we should pray for as we ought.*

The words of the prayer kept rehearsing in my memory and I really didn't have a clue why I was so intrigued. I was able to recite it to myself without looking at the paper; I mediated on the words and even envisioned myself applying them to situations in an imaginary state. Little did I know that in time to come, I would be tested of the very same words and would have to apply all that I had repeatedly meditated on firsthand in my own life.

Is the valley season an answer to the prayer I prayed? let me share my valley season with you and together we will figure it out. *Behold, I send you forth as sheep in the midst of wolves: be ye therefore wise as serpents, and harmless as doves;* Matthew 10:16.

The unknown author of an excerpt that was introduced to me quite a while after I first read the prayer suggests; *"much that perplexes us in our experience is but the answer to our prayers. We pray for patience, and our Father sends those who tax us to the utmost; for "tribulation worketh patience". We pray for submission, and God sends sufferings; for "we learn obedience by the things we suffer". We pray for unselfishness, and God gives us opportunities to sacrifice ourselves by thinking on the things of others, and by laying down our lives for the brethren. We pray for strength and humility, and some messenger of Satan torments us until we lie in the dust crying for its removal. We pray for gentleness, and there comes a perfect storm of temptation to harshness and irritability. We pray for quietness, and every nerve is strung to the utmost tension, so that looking to Him we may learn that when He giveth quietness, no one can make trouble. We pray for love, and God sends peculiar suffering and puts us with apparently unlovely people, and lets them say things which rasp the nerves and lacerate the heart; for love suffereth long and is kind, love is not impolite, love is not provoked. LOVE BEARETH ALL THINGS, believeth, hopeth and endureth, love never faileth."*

I have experienced tremendous growth in my spirituality and personhood, and you will see that I have articulated my thoughts as they related to my personal spiritual values and my life on a whole. With extremely high regard, I recognized God working in and through me. I realized the Spirit of God as my source and resource and in total surrender I practiced my spirituality through reverence, obedience and intimacy with Almighty God.

Quotes from known and unknown, living and deceased legends of speeches and writings are referenced in this book. These excerpts brought timely convictions, repentance, restoration and redemption to me that I would like to share with the universe. By combining my story and the quotes I used in this season, my desire is to see practical results of victory from the challenges you face, so you may be amongst the forerunners for the next generation. I purposely included these quotes as I would like you to know that wisdom and insight can be enhanced or gained by turning to those who have already hacked a trail through the jungle of experiences and ideas.

The focus of this story is to highlight the good that can result from situations that were intended to harm. Arni Jacobson states in his book, The Favor Factor, *"If someone isn't attacking you, there is a good chance you are not doing anything that is worth worrying the opposition".* I personally believe we must rid ourselves from limited, shallow thinking, look beyond circumstances and situations, and find purpose and actualize our potentials consciously in an effort to see tangible results individually, then corporately; thus, the logo "world-changer" can be modeled.

CHAPTER 1

DISCOVERY

"Be careful what you wish for, you just might get it", the challenge lies in the process, but at the end of the journey "you get it". The consequences may be disappointing, but sometimes before appointment, there comes disappointment. One speaker said it this way, *"the way to peace and victory is to accept every circumstance, every trial, straight from the hand of the loving Father; and to live up in the heavenly places, above the clouds, in the very presence of the throne, and to look down from the glory upon our environment as lovingly and divinely appointed."* unknown. One of the most conscious discoveries I made, was that in life things just don't happen, they existed before I became aware; **awareness conveys revelation**.

While at peace with myself and everyone and everything around me, without putting out an effort, I met a man, [I will call him Jacob], who appeared to be the perfect gentleman, with physical gestures and just an overall demeanor that seemed to be one-of-a-kind. He showed qualities similar to the perfect husband material, showing much interest in me and more importantly my son, Ryanne. We dated for quite sometimes and with him, I experienced some of the best wining and dining, charisma, and charm; you name it, he had it. I thought to myself, I have been single from my last meaningful relationship for five and a half years and as everyone around me would ask, when will you meet your significant other to have a father figure for your son? That was the common talk and it got to pressuring me and I sometimes thought that if Ryanne was growing up according to society's standards, he would *need* a male figure in his life to be a complete child. My dad died when I was at an early age in my childhood and in my immediate household, I had no man to use as reference or guide. My extended male family, cousins and uncles, lived in other geographic regions and being that my mother raised my three sisters and I, I became very independent at an early age and was comfortable taking care of myself and my son.

As our friendship grew and time passed, one Friday evening, while enjoying dinner at a very upscale restaurant, he looked me in the eyes, took my hand and in a stutter asked me if I would be his bride. I was shocked as this was least expected, but with a big grin I accepted the ring which was too big for my finger. Man, I thought to myself, he proposed to me, I didn't even have to sweat it; but a strange feeling came over me, I lost my appetite and I became nervous. I wasn't sure what it was, I knew for sure that I was over my last relationship and I was as free as a bird, so what could it be? I trusted my instincts, but felt as if I needed a mature person's views on the way I felt.

A very good friend of mine who knew of our relationship and to whom I confided in, called me as I got home the evening and I told her of the good news. My only concern was that deep in my soul, I was not at peace about accepting the proposal. My friend who we will call Jill was older and had been married to the same man for thirty-five plus years, so I trusted that her insights would be accurate. Jill was thrilled to hear of the good news and after a few minutes of conversation, I told her of my true inner feelings which was that everything seemed to be going well with Jacob, but I didn't have a sense of peace in my spirit about going forward with him. The one thing Jill mentioned was his attitude towards Ryanne was above average and that was true. She was a witness as he made it possible for me to be involved in social groups and he would find events for children and would often take Ryanne. As I listened to Jill's views and exchanged thoughts, the response from Jill was that "no one is perfect" and what she saw was good so I should go for it. Anyway, while the ultimate decision was mine, I forced myself into ignoring my inner-feelings; what a mistake!

When I invited Jacob to a fellowship, the reaction from the people was not very warm, but as I could see only what I saw, I tried not to question the opinions of others. We took counseling classes by a minister of his choice and even though I was not comfortable, my own weakness got the best of me and I decided to let the man be the man just because he showed much kindness and interest. The Sunday before we decided on the marriage arrangements, we visited a Church in our neighborhood and the one outstanding thing that got my attention to the heart and soul was an excerpt read by the minister and I thought of Jacob and the stories he told of his misfortunes. I hand wrote these words in a "Thinking of You" card and gave it to him with a promise, only because I believed his stories; later I found out that they were all polished lies. I refer to him as Jacob as the name translates to "*deceit*"

I must use this for some personal benefit and share it with others, and so, with agape, I now dedicate this to *you* as everyone deserves understanding:

> *Because I see your past, I celebrate your progress;*
> *- "Everyone is worth understanding"*
> *Because I see your plan, I understand your problem*
> *Because I see your peculiarity, I accept your personality*
> *Because I see your potential, I believe in your promise*
> *Because I see your purpose, I comprehend your passion*
> *Because I see your power, I have faith in your possibilities*
> *Because I see your place [in life], I will help you find your path* [unknown]

I was a full-time student pursuing a master's degree, working professional, volunteer at community organizations, full-time mom and wife, yet I was completely empty – I just could not figure it out. We were having good times, but through it all, it didn't feel as though we were on the same accord and I was very uncomfortable. Over a period, going on two years in the marriage, I discovered some hidden issues that Jacob was dealing with that were very disappointing, but I got a relief in my spirit that confirmed that my initial feelings were accurate. After discussing with him my beliefs and values as they related to the issues, he apologized and did all the visual things to convince me that his apology was sincere, but he didn't truly change.

Jacob suddenly changed his countenance and attitude towards our relationship and would often appear to be guilty after he got caught, he didn't' seem to have forgiven himself even though I empathized with him. As I knew deep down that I had forgiven him and was willing to work with him on seeking counsel for recovery, it really was not a big deal to me that he had unresolved personal issues; it was revealed and needed to be dealt with. I had a busy schedule but would often suggest that he sought counseling from reliable sources for recovery and would make time to discuss our future as it related to the matter. His reactions always seem to be defensive and he appeared to suffer from a guilty conscience, but I didn't see the reason for his odd behavior as I truly cared about him and our relationship; I then became suspicious. It turned out that he was not sincere about his confessions and was exposed as a chronic liar with a deceiving way of handling his secrets when revealed.

We were not always on the same accord as we had slightly different cultural and spiritual beliefs. Jacob was raised in another faith and was later converted to Christianity and while we attended church together regularly, he didn't seem to handle convictions well. While working at resolving those issues, they got worst. After I had exhausted all my options, I referred him to a class that was geared towards people with similar issues he struggled with, but he disagreed. When I advised him that unless he made an effort to improve, the marriage would be dissolved because of the stress it caused me, he grudgingly agreed to counseling. After a series of counseling with an older veteran minister that proved futile, the real Jacob was revealed. The counselor's words that pierced my entire being were "*you picked up something deadly, but it didn't harm you, go in peace, and do not be ashamed as you were hit on the blind side."*

When reality hits, what do you do? live with it, face it, rise above it.

I became angry at myself and wondered of the necessary steps to take toward restoration. I thought about the decision that I was about to make several times and clearly saw in many ways that Jacob's struggles far outweighed his kindness and the issue at hand was not on the surface; Jacob needed to work on himself for himself with his own decision. I took Ryanne for a snack that afternoon and told him that I made a terrible mistake in marrying Jacob and asked him to forgive me. He was only thirteen, but understood and was very supportive.

While rearranging my closet for my seasonal wear in preparation for the fall, I saw a book bag on the shelf that I had not looked at in a long time. As I searched through the bag, I came across a file folder with an assignment that I had completed in a "Student's

Success Skills" seminar when pursuing my bachelor's degree. Immediately, the thought of my purpose, goals and personal development became of great concern. "**I must face reality in action**", I thought, and so I pulled out a folder with some incomplete writings that I started just after Ryanne's birth and began to read them back to myself. As I pondered on these mixed events, I thought, this is the opportunity to tell it to God Himself; not that He needed to know, but because I needed to hear His response. As I developed dialogue with the Almighty, I could clearly see, hear and feel His responses, the still small voice whispered, "Time to go."

J. R. Miller an authentic person of faith, once said:
*"there are times when we are to go forward with a firm step. There are many divine promises which are conditioned upon the beginning of some action on our part. When we begin to obey, God will begin to bless us. Great things were promised to Abraham, but not one of them could have been obtained by waiting in Chaldea. He must leave home, friends, and country, and go out into **unknown** paths and **press** on in unfaltering obedience in order to receive the promises. The ten lepers were told to show themselves to the priest, and '**as they went they were cleansed**", if they had waited to see the cleansing come in their flesh before they would start, they would never have seen it. God was waiting to cleanse them; and the moment their faith began to work, the blessing came.*
When the Israelites were shut in by a pursuing army at the Red Sea, they were commanded to "Go Forward". The key to unlock the gate into the land of promise they held in their own hands, and the gate would not turn on its hinges until they had approached it and unlocked it. That key was faith. Press forward with bold confidence and take what is yours."

I knew I needed a change of scene; but where? I had many choices, but was suffering from so much emotional reproach, I felt as though I disappointed my family, friends and mostly my child. After I decided to relocate, a few days before submitting my resignation at work, to my surprise, a week later, a co-worker sent me an email that had the very same contents of my thoughts towards my purpose. She walked over to my desk and we discussed the contents of the email and she advised me that the first person that came to her mind was me when she read it. Prior to her sending me this email, we never talked about my personal vision and I knew that it was confirmation of my plan; I was then reminded of the star in me and told myself. -"***twinkle, twinkle***" *.

I Discover Myself

Through intense self-evaluation, I gained a better understanding of my purpose and became more aware of my personal vision. When I became conscious of my state-of-being and I realized that I lowered my standards in some of the choices I made, I immediately repented, regained my grounds, raised the standard of my faith, the standard of my living in God's kingdom and the standard of my expectations.

I constantly reminded myself that God's will for me is to excel and to live a balanced life by His grace and His direction. At this point, I began to see myself as fearfully and wonderfully made by the Creator of the universe as mentioned in the Holy Scriptures, thus, I started to gain spiritual strength, just as David did when he gained strength in his days of adversity.

I would often speak to myself and tell myself that "I am more than mere flesh and blood, I am spirit and the power of my spirit connected to God's Spirit has supernatural power and presence that I can live in and will bring victory over all adversity. I am designed for victory and I belong to God. I have decided to follow God's path, walk in the Spirit knowing that I will be triumphant."

- *"Failed relationships may be futile, but life and love are not final". -* **Sophia**

Where did I go wrong? I trusted Jacob upfront and didn't take the time to seek proper guidance. I also made decisions based on his terms and forced myself into ignoring my inner-feelings.

How I handle my mistake

I was honest with myself and faced reality with action. My focus was on restoration and my future and I was not worried about the past. I had to ignore the views and comments of judgmental and ignorant people around me and reminded myself that "he who feels it, knows it". I am in agreement with Wayne Dyer's views on handling issues of such and would rather quote this eloquent piece he wrote than to say it any other way: *"All blame is a waste of time. No matter how much fault you find with another, and regardless of how much you blame him, it will not change you. The only thing blame does is to keep the focus off you when you are looking for external reasons to explain your unhappiness or frustration. You may succeed in making another feel guilty about something by blaming him, but you won't succeed in changing whatever it is about you that are making you unhappy."* .

As an open-minded, fearless person, I took on a personal assignment to seek change in the direction that my life was going as I knew my destiny depended on how I handled this particular situation. I was rather moved by the following words by King Whitney, Jr.

"***Change*** *has a considerable psychological impact on the human mind. To the fearful it is threatening because it means that things may get worse. To the hopeful it is encouraging because things may get better. To the confident it is **inspiring** because the challenge exists to **make things better**."*

CHAPTER 2

JOURNEY THROUGH THE VALLEY

Faith and Facts

"Difficulty is sent to reveal to us what God can do in answer to the faith that prays and works. Are you straitened in the valleys? Get away to the hills, live there; get honey out of the rock, and wealth out of the terraced slopes now hidden by forest." – Daily Devotional Commentary.

Again, the human side became weak; ashamed and disappointed, I thought the best thing to do was to call it "one of those things" and move on. [I had to keep encouraging myself] I was also reminded "no pain, no gain" *and would tell myself, "you are a winner, Sophia - your name means wisdom from above".* Calling on the God of Wisdom became my favorite prayer; I got clear direction to relocate which was later confirmed from several sources, and there after an unexpected door became open. I headed to a city where a friend of my relative was desperate for a roommate as she had just relocated from another city and was alone in a newly purchased home.

The peace that passes all understanding was at work. Upon my arrival, the homeowner greeted me pleasantly and commended me on my boldness, and was happy that I made it in safe. While I was not insecure or intimidated, emotional distress began to creep upon me as everyone was worried about my where about - my mother became extremely concerned and worrisome and I began hurting in every way, "your life is going down the drain" were her words as I ended a very short telephone conversation in anger. She had such frustration in her voice and so I began to cry and think; I must come to a point of restoration.

The next day, I found out that the homeowner was experiencing financial challenges and was desperate to pay her bills. She was not able to meet her mortgage payment as there was a salary difference and her income was much less than before. She contended that her husband was not settled in a job, and told story after story. I thought to myself, God, I don't need this. I cannot bear someone else's burden when I have enough of my own.

Things didn't work out as anticipated based upon the agreement with the home-owner. When I told her of my profession and she overheard a telephone conversation I held with a recruiter as I quoted my minimum salary, she called around to someone who shared the same profession to inquiry about my salary range, and since then had a demand for more money.

I went searching for a place of my own and rented an apartment where I was scheduled to move in the next month. I was not totally satisfied about moving to this apartment as it was within a few miles from the county line from the school district. Due to restrictions related to the school district and residence, it was not the best choice to move my son the third time in such short period as he was in the middle of the semester when we relocated and he had just begin settling in this school. It was stressful to think of how to handle this as I would have to find a way to get Ryanne to school so that he could complete the semester and my only other option was to place him in yet another school; this only added more to the emotional pain. I could no longer tolerate this lady's behavior and I chose to ignore the conversations that came up around her indebtedness and then announced to her that I would be moving at the end of the month which was five weeks in her home and I had spent a large sum of money on food and lodging which was almost twice my monthly expenses when I lived in my own home.

As I entered an electronics store to have my cellular phone converted to the local area code, I met a couple who invited me to a cultural celebration that lasted for an extended period. I told them that I was new in town and thought it was a good idea to learn the local culture and experience the social and civic activities. Two days later, my son and I visited the event, but as it was dismissed rather late, I told the host who seemed very friendly that with respect to the home that I was staying, I did not want to be going in and out of someone's house that late; her response was not very pleasant.

A week later, I attended a conference type fellowship and sat beside a lady, [I will call her Pam] that seemed personable; we greeted each other and talked a few minutes before the program began. We realized that our homes were in the same general area and Pam suggested that we exchanged numbers. Two days later while returning from an interview, I received a call from Pam and she invited me to visit with her. Upon arrival at her house, she asked me to accompany her to the nearby mall and so we both went. On our way, she began telling me of her past profession and the various misfortunes that came her way. In return, I opened up and told her that I had just relocated from another city, newly separated, trying to put the past behind and get settled. As we decided to attend the conference for the time that it lasted, she suggested car pooling as we lived in the same general area and it would be beneficial to both of us and I agreed.

After a few times of hanging out with Pam, she mentioned that since I am new in town, unsettled and we were both single parents, the "Lord told her" that she should open her home to me until I get settled. At this time, her house was approximately six miles from where I lived. I mentioned my concern for having to transfer my son to another school at this stage and I didn't feel that it was the right choice. She insisted that I stayed with her for the time as she was trying to get herself established with a home-based business that she had recently started and it would benefit us both as we were trying to get grounded. Pam referenced the fact that we are both single parents and it would be good if we could help each other. I had no objection, but I was very direct in telling her that if I were to live with her it would be for a very short moment as I was accustomed to living as part of or head of my household and I wanted to keep my son in the school district.

One evening while we were on our way to the grocery store in Pam's car, I received a phone call from the apartment contact where I signed a lease, wanting to confirm my move-in date. I told her that I changed my mind, "you mean you are going to let your non-refundable deposit go like that"; I responded by telling her that I got a better deal. As the agent attempted to negotiate a better deal than she had originally offered me, Pam interjected and said, you are new and you need to know the area first. Without much thought and since I had to move in to the apartment by a certain date and just the thought of possibly breaking a lease, I thought, Pam might just be God sent, so I decided to take her up on her offer. Giving her the benefit of the doubt, as she mentioned that her mortgage payment would be short due to unexpected issues, prior to moving in to her place on December 1, I paid her five hundred dollars in cash.

Days went by and I accepted a position in a downtown law firm as a contract paralegal where I met another lady who lived one street away from Ryanne's school in the neighborhood where I first lived. As we began talking I realized her son was class-mates with Ryanne and we decided to car-pool. She offered for Ryanne to ride the school bus with her son and that went in our favor and I was relieved from concerns of such.

After I moved in with Pam, I realized that she lied about her source of income and she was involved with a man that she was trying to end the relationship. She confessed to me that my renting from her will cover the bills that this man would pay and she would not have any other reason to see him. I was disappointed as I didn't expect to hear that and thought it was perhaps a wrong move to take up on her offer. As mentioned before, Pam's temperament seemed very warm and I couldn't image her not being sincere as she appeared very kind and concerned.

While I was away at work during the day, Pam was searching through my belongings and corresponding with people who saw us together about all kinds of ill-will towards me. She would often repeat things about herself and chose to point the finger at me. At times, she would seem to be looking for a reason to compare her with my situation as if she was trying to find something in common with me or my weak spot to prey on. She often reminded me of the challenges that I faced; as I am a strong-spirited person by nature, I would often advise her that I am looking ahead as the past is history. She couldn't seem to fathom the strength I had in such challenging times, and would often remind me of how sad my situation was and she stated that perhaps she was the best person around that would open her home to me. She tried to play a fake pity party and would often prey on the fact that I was separated and I would tell her of my views as they relate to life in its real sense; this seemed extremely challenging to Pam as her games would often return to her.

One day after the conference was dismissed, while I was waiting on Pam as she was talking with a lady, who repeated all that she heard to other sources, which usually found its way to the facilitators of the conference, I gave a lady a compliment on her attire and we started a conversation. She returned the compliment to me on my hair cut and I told her I was preparing for a job interview. She then asked me of my profession and I told her that I worked in the legal field. She advised me that she knew of a law firm that was hiring and recommended that I contact them. Within a few days of submitting my resume, I received a call from the company's human resources for an interview. I was hired for a permanent job and began working with the law firm a month after.

My emotions were being tampered with as people who were ignorant of the situation, favored Pam and without verifying the information, they sided with her and would reference the information as a means to subdue me. I immediately thought that I was on a journey that felt like "*the valley*" and so the most optimistic thing to think of was that I must make it a point to have "joy" in the midst of it all. In order to be my own consoler, I became grateful of the newly found job that was similar to the position that I held at my last place of employment. I now had a notable reason for the joy as when Pam was sowing discord against me and baring false tales, God was using another person to bless me in a way I could not imagine. **"You see clear with your heart; visibility is not always essential".**

After a few days at Pam's house, I noticed that she was not tidy and seemed to be looking for a maid to clean up after her. Pam began showing her true colors and would often assign Ryanne to house chores that would include cleaning up after her and her daughter, while her daughter would be on the internet. When I confronted Pam, she would tell me that she was raised by people who ill-treated her and I asked her very aggressively not to repeat the same with my son. I also told her I would not allow this, as the agreement was that I rented and paid to be at her place. Again, in her subtle treacherous way, she tried to remind me that she invited me in her home and I directly told her that upon moving in her home, I paid her to stay as well as bought healthy food and contributed to her bills. When I advised her that I will not be at her home for more than the time I needed to be there, her attitude towards me changed and the tales multiplied.

I Evaluate Myself

Relative to my condition at that time, I knew that I was on the right path. The faith that lies within me kept me going as nothing in the visible was looking favorable. The challenge was chartering the "unknown"; if God is with me, why worry? Why not embark on the journey ahead?

The facts and current conditions around me kept showing up more visible than the blessings that were present, I knew at this point that it was totally up to me to decide how I would handle these issues. I must run my own race, I thought; so, I refused to allow my emotions to take over and throw me into a tailspin. My focus was to allow the anointing of my destiny to flow, to be that chosen one; that called one and exercise a brand-new faith in the Day of God's power.

"*The odds are for me*", became my personal statement. During times of turmoil and seasons of extremes, I was able to find stability as I trusted the source of my existence [God]. I believed I was at a point in my life where it was vitally important for me to exercise my personal will to see beyond other people's short-comings and let God handle the situations.

Did I make the right choice in relocating to a place where I had the least amount of friends and relatives? "The *Unknown*"

*"It takes a lot of courage to release the familiar and seemingly secure, to embrace the new. But there is no real security in what is no longer meaningful. There is more security in the **adventurous** and **exciting**, for in **movement** there is **life**, and in **change** there is **power**."* - Alan Cohen

I am a risk taker by nature and I thought of the unknown as being fertile ground and a place to start over where I could be productive. I felt that I needed to be free from the known as I feared stagnation. I knew life had more to offer than the challenges that I experienced and I did not want the known to place me in the prison of past conditioning. With an optimistic view on life, I thought to myself that sometimes the disappointment comes before the appointment, so I pressed on into the unknown with the mustard seed faith believing to move mountains. I then remembered the email that I received, revisited it and after meditating on the words, I believed it was confirmation.

Sophia Rios

From: Tyra Conwell
Sent: Wednesday, September 24, 2003 9:15 AM
To: 'careerwoman@msn.com'; Sophia Rios; 'harrisv123@aol.com'
Subject: For Today!!!

DAILY DEVOTIONAL: SEPTEMBER 24, 2003
I WILL BLESS THE FAMILIES OF THE EARTH THROUGH YOU

Today's Scripture Reading:
Galatians 3:26-29; Genesis 12:1-7

Key Verse:
Genesis 12:1-3

Prayer Tools

Tools for Prayer

Daily Devotional
Food For Thought
Prayer Requests
Nuggets of Faith
On Evangelism

Nuggets of Faith

Reward is Certain
Like Palm & Cedar
Complete Safety
Reason for Singing
Perfect Willingness

Get out of your country, From your family And from your father's house, To a land that I will show you. I will make you a great nation;
I will bless you And make your name great; And you shall be a blessing.
I will bless those who bless you, And I will curse him who curses you;
And in you all the families of the earth shall be blessed.

Abraham was more than a man whom God greatly blessed. He also was a blessing to others because of God's promise: "I will make you a great nation: / I will bless you / And make your name great; / And you shall be a blessing." What did God do to Abraham in this verse? He identified the call and purpose of Abram with His call and purpose according to His own schedule and agenda. It would not happen because Abram wanted it to happen; it came to pass God's way.

God still wants to bless all the families of the earth through His kingdom. For that reason, He has to remove us from the familiar to prepare us for the unthinkable and the miraculous.

Most of us in the church are disjointed from the corporate move of God. The truth is that if your vision does not identify with God's overall plan, then it is a "wish-ion." Many are still stuck in the rut of Genesis 12:1 - they have not left the "home" of the familiar and the comfortable, and they refuse to separate from the trappings of the past. Others are stuck in Genesis 12:2; they constantly remind us how God is blessing them long before we see any fruit in their lives. Very few reach the heart of the matter in Genesis 12:3, where they understand that everything happens because God has an overall plan for the salvation of the world-and He wants to demonstrate it through our physical and spiritual families.

Think about it in perspective: you are the beginning of a divine plan and eternal kingdom that does not stop at your grave! It flows through your physical and spiritual bloodline on an eternal journey of glory and wonder.

What an awesome privilege we have in Jesus Christ! Pray this prayer with me:

Holy Father, thank You for including me in the inheritance of the kingdom through Jesus Christ. Now I can pass along the anointing, blessing, and destiny of the call to my children and my children's children. Thank you, Father, Amen.

9/24/2003

CHAPTER 3

IN THE VALLEY

"For a great door and effectual is opened unto me, and there are many adversaries" **1ST Corinthians 16 vs. 9**

"Afflictions are often the black folds in which God doth set the jewels of His children's graces, to make them shine the better." Unknown.

The load had been heavy and my heart burdened which created a spiritual fog so that I was not able to see clearly where I was headed or where to take my next step. I then gradually began to release my burdens to God in order to gain clarity. I thought I must wait for God to unfold His plans and provision and was careful not to do anything by force of my own logic and will. I refused to be discouraged or to be in a state of despair as I could see God guiding me and bringing me through the obstructions that the enemy has devised against me.

I believe that in order for my graces to be discovered, God often sends me trials, that I may be witness of the existence. As I became aware of my stand in the journey, I realized that real growth in grace is not just discovered, it is practical, relevant occurrences with substantial improvement in life that result in inner-peace, freedom and balance.
I have been called trooper by many and am well aware that intense training in any area of life requires surrendering to God, personal development,

discipline, will-power and purpose. In order to smile at the storm or to have joy in the valley, I would have to learn the hard way to deal with first hand traitors, misrepresentation; I would have to look them in the face with love and keep on moving. Unkind remarks from different sources were passed after false rumors were circulated. I was not insulted, I had already learned that before I obtain a promise, I would have to personally experience many adversarial schemes and plots and learn purpose, and so, it was not difficult for me to take this as caution.

I do not suffer with low self-esteem and have always submitted to authority within reasoning, and in observing strong foundations, I have learned that people who are considered legends must be prepared to overcome many challenges. This then became a reality to me that pressure has to come and challenges will present themselves to people who have something to offer to the universe. The greatest of it all is to know that *it will not prevail.*

One of the things that were attractive about Pam was her appearance; her approach, tone and her gestures seemed warm and she appeared to be personable. Pam held good professional positions in corporate settings and was able to afford a good lifestyle, but she told me that several months before we met, she lost her job. She mentioned that her entire world had changed and she was not coping very well with life as it was. Pam was older than me and would often reference my age and tell me that when she was my age she was not as serious about life and settled as I. We had very little in common; the one thing we had in common was that we were both single parents.

Our approach to life was very different, she was very soft spoken and often used euphemisms, while I was direct and to the point which sometimes appeared to be insensitive to her. As I am somewhat thick-skinned, the one thing I learned from Pam and practiced since then, was to consider thin skinned, overly sensitive individuals. I got to meet a few of Pam's associates and realized that they appeared to suffer from inferiority-superiority complex which confirmed to me that I was amongst the wrong crowd.

Petty, trifling behavior was not attractive to me and seemed to be the norm in Pam's circle of friends. She often spoke of her childhood and seemed to have harbored resentment in her heart against the people who raised her. I thought of my own personal childhood memories that I wished didn't exist; my dad died when I was very young, that was something that I couldn't help, but I don't hold a grudge against anyone for such tragedy that life dished. Pam and I had many different beliefs related to basic lifestyles and the approach we took in life, she was not the typical woman who cooked, or did house chores or even spent time with her daughter mainly because of her prior work schedule and her mid-life crisis.

I am a vegetarian and am selective with my diet. My favorite dishes are food from the earth like sweet potatoes, green vegetables and creatures of the sea. I enjoy home-cooked meals and one of the dishes that I love to cook is cod fish. Cod fish doesn't always have a pleasant smell as it is very salty and when boiled can give off a salty-raw smell. While preparing a dish with codfish and spinach, Pam became grossly judgmental and I thought, how close minded can one be? We went to the grocery store and I bought fruits, vegetables and food for the house and she was surprised at my choosing organic food over the processed, frozen food.

In the shopping plaza was an oriental store, and I walked over to purchase some herbal teas. At the entrance of the shop were a *cross* and a *picture of Jesus and his followers seated around the table*, and this confirmed to me that these people had similar spiritual beliefs as I. This was a shop where the Asian owner practiced herbal medicine and acupuncture; his patients would complete a form and he would examine them. I asked the doctor of his background and he got defensive. A few moments later, I found out that he was very well-known in the community. I then apologized and advised him that the reason for my asking was that I was new in town and I wanted to know who I was allowing to serve me. He then lightened up and showed me write-ups on his practice in the local newspaper. I was asked to extend my hand and he checked my pulse, looked in my eyes and my mouth, just like a regular doctor.

He charged me five dollars for the examination in addition to the cost for the herbs. He then mixed four different herbs and gave me the instructions to prepare the tea. Pam also got herself checked as she said she was interested in losing weight and wanted to try the herbs for weight loss.

While leaving the shop, Pam mentioned that the Asian's ancestors were superstitious and that she was un-comfortable being there. I told her that I was there only for the herbs and the world is full of superstition, so I wouldn't pick any special group of people and out of ignorance and prejudice choose to stereotype or label them as anything; and besides, why did she ask for service for her weight loss. She then began with a long conversation based on cultural prejudices and I thought to myself; not again Lord, another major mistake? While unpacking the groceries, I used vinegar to wash my fruits before putting them away and Pam commented on how strange I was. Again, a small voice reminded me that this is a test and I would think of the words, *'where there is darkness; light"* – *St. Francis' prayer.*

"The mind is like a parachute; it functions better when opened". – Unknown.

Pam simply needed to open her mind. One day while Pam and I were discussing general issues related to society, she told me that my views seemed strange to her and so, to improve her limited thinking, I thought of sharing a series of teachings by Chip Ingram a well-known speaker who had a series of teaching entitled "*The Invisible War*". While searching through the box with my books, tapes and writings, she saw some of the writings that I had produced and I mentioned that I had a passion for the arts and that the majority of my writings were stored on my laptop.

Through conversation, I shared a part of my vision with Pam as she spoke about her home-based business and how she would like me to give her tips on marketing techniques and how to improve her services, and I did. I picked the cassettes from the package and we both listened to the speaker. Pam seemed puzzled, and then she confessed that she was discussing me with people in the community because she thought something was strange about me, but she now saw that I am very mature for my age. She also told me that she was jealous and thought that she should have been more productive in her earlier years – at last the truth came out.

A few days went by and Pam invited me to accompany her to a fellowship conducted by an elderly couple at the same venue of the conference where we met. I went and thought it was similar to the community festival that I attended previously, so without hesitation, I invited her and she came. Again, Pam became critical and fault finding of the type of activities as she was not familiar with the cultural performances. I thought to myself that Pam needed exposure and need to take an open approach to different behavior and activities. I couldn't help but directly advise her that people are creatures of their environment and can only behave according to what they know and the world does not evolve around one particular person, place or thing; it is everyone and the various environments combined that make up the earth. Again, this was twisted and the ethnocentric folks interpreted it with a narrow mind-set.

Pam would often uttered negative remarks related to people's views if they were contrary to hers and when I suggested embracing other cultures and different activities, we would often end up disagreeing. When she made the negative remarks of the people's behavior, I reminded her that the event she invited me to that we attended prior to the one she accompanied me were exactly the same; the only difference was the demographics, structure and locations. Pam then told me that she purposely avoided her relatives in the city where she came from as they were all involved into weird traditional rituals and when she saw behavior that were unfamiliar, she was reminded of them and would become judgmental.

During the conversation, I told Pam that in my childhood years, I was never exposed to any weird ritualistic custom, but once when I was a young adult, I visited a well-known theme park in a major city where I lived and had my palm read. This was in the open where major crowds gathered, so I didn't think anything weird of it as I believe that when people are engaging in known negative rituals, they usually don't do it in public places. I learned after that it was not in-line with my spiritual beliefs and since then repented as it was done out of curiosity and ignorance.

Later that night, Pam was retrieving her email and sure enough, she was communicating with several psychics via email – confirmation. My words to her were, "*IT NEVER FAILS; AS A MAN THINKETH, SO IS HE;* if one doesn't know of something, his conclusion may be a reflection of his own deeds or familiar environment". It was rather a coincidence that within a few minutes of the conversation, we were watching a broadcast hosted by a well-known speaker and a few seconds of the broadcast the host referenced the very same words, "*as a man thinks in his heart, so is he*" and "*we see things the way we are*". Pam and I were shocked as it seemed as if the speaker was included in the conversation and she immediately confessed to me that she was convicted. I told her that I am not perfect myself but echoed the statement not as condemnation but as a statement of reality. This was about the second week at Pam's home and I then decided that it was time for me to go as I was not accustomed to this type of lifestyle and was rather uncomfortable. During the week while I was at work, Pam contacted some of the people we met at the community festival and began with the same rumors she started before.

"*Our spiritual conflicts are among our choicest blessings, and our greatest adversary is used to train us for his ultimate defeat. Just as the wise sailor can use a head wind to carry him forward by tacking and taking advantage of its impelling force; so it is possible for us in our spiritual life through the victorious grace of God to turn to account the things that seem most unfriendly and unfavorable, and to be able to say continually, "The things that were against me have happened to the furtherance of my benefit"* – excerpt taken from life more abundantly.

One day while I was about to retrieve a document from my laptop, I realized that I couldn't get it to work after several attempts of trying to turn it on. I recalled the last time I retrieved documents from the laptop was two days before moving in with Pam, and the people at the first house were not computer literate; whatever went wrong, must have happened while I was in transition. When I mentioned to Pam that my laptop was broken, she questioned how it happened and I told her I didn't know, but someone tampered with it since I came to her home. She became defensive and pointed out that she is the homeowner and she would not need to interfere with my laptop as I am the person who is in her home. I reminded her that I was not homeless, I was in transition and she stepped in and offered me to share with her, plus she was paid upfront for the time that I lodged at her house.

A few days later, we visited a fellowship service at the invitation of Pam's neighbor. The speaker was referencing the abuse and deception of possession and how a common trait of insecure people was to use their positions and possessions as a way of denying their cruel deeds and weaknesses and prey on others. After the service, Pam then began making reference to the very people to whom she sought refuge that were defending her. Little did they know that she was a first class traitor; it was later discovered that Pam was feeding information to sources that repeated the gossip, but twisted it all to seem like an innocent person.

In a few days, the false rumors multiplied amongst the people that saw me in her company, as the tales were recycled to paint the worst imaginable picture of me; I was not moved - I said to myself "*love never fails*". When I heard the tales repeated that were told by Pam, I thought to myself that my conscience was clear and I had no reason to worry or defend myself. *"In this will I be confident"*, were the words that kept rehearsing in my heart, at this time, I no longer felt like a victim, but saw the opportunity to become a victor. Chuck Pierce, a classic world speaker and minister suggests in his book God's Now Time For your Life that *"if you know God has placed you where you are, even if it seems like Babylon, stay there as long as God asks"; it is either one of these two questions that will bring the answer, "who put you where you are; why are you there".* My conclusion; "THIS IS A TEST".

"Time for another change", I said to myself. Changes are inevitable, but I know I can make the necessary adjustments easily if I trust God to take me through this time of transition, even though I felt that I had to bear the brunt of responsibility, God was with me every step of the way and I refused to allow fear to overtake me.

The harder the conflict, the more glorious the triumph. What we obtain too cheap, we esteem too lightly; it is dearness only that gives everything its value. I love the man that can smile in trouble that can gather strength from distress and grow brave by reflection. 'Tis the business of little minds to shrink; but he whose heart is firm, and whose conscience approves his conduct, will pursue his principles unto death". – **Thomas Paine**

I purposed in my heart to see the glass half-full and told myself that the other half is making room for more. Another person's lies, biased-truths, labels or personal beliefs will not hinder me from accomplishing my goals and so I press towards that which I see in the invisible. I began counting my blessings and naming them, I was alive, well, had everything I needed; not quite satisfied, but hoped that the season would soon expire. *"Hope itself is like a star – not to be seen in the sunshine of prosperity, and only to be discovered in the night of adversity,* **says C.H. Spurgeon, so I started to refer to myself as the girl with hope**. *"Count your blessings. Once you realize how valuable you are and how much you have going for you, the smiles will return, the sun will break out, the music will play, and you will finally be able to move forward the life that God intended for you with grace, strength, courage and confidence."* Og. Mandion

As time passed and individuals were coached to provoke me with some of the things that I encountered between Pam and the folks who defended her, I often felt the need to retaliate and tell the truth of the matter. It was rather painful and unfortunate, but I believe when it is one person's words against another, people will always believe who or what they want to believe for their own personal reasons and I didn't see the need to engage in a "tug-o-war". One of Pam's friends would often relay issues related to her deep dirty secrets that I knew of and I would sometimes think that I should indeed throw that in her face, but I would be convicted before and decided not to repeat them.

When I thought of how to handle the situation; I had mixed feelings. I was then reminded of one theory that my grandma instilled in me while growing up, "people's homes are their private belongings and it is out of order to visit people's homes and carry out their intimate dirt to the street." I also believe that people who look for dirty laundry are like the laundry mat or the cleaners; think of it, the folks who operate the dry cleaners never expose their own dirt, because they are the cleaning people, but they operate businesses to clean others laundry. My exposing Pam's dirty laundry would not and have not benefited me; she created lasting damage that only the folks involved know the true details of the matter. I did not need to tell about her or anyone else to feel secure in any manner, even though sometimes I caught myself telling some of the issues I encountered which tied into her actions.

The interesting fact was that time revealed to us all that Pam was talking about her own hidden issues that haunted her and she was only trying to pass the buck and had to point the finger. As I went along, I realized that Pam seemed to be more of a personality than a person that was used as means of extracting information from others who strive to be above mediocrity. Through all this, I know destiny is a journey and God gives graces and anointing which empowers me to face the extremes of this season and to arise for His purpose. My portion is to believe God will work out all the details. I rested in peace and assurance knowing that God was working on my behalf, and the good work that God began in me will be brought to completion.

An amusing poem by *Maya Angelo,* one of my favorite poets, a living legend of poetry and literature was sent to me through email and I thought of the truth it brings, her amusing writing style and how it relates to the many challenges that I faced in this season. I am free-spirited and liberal; smiling at the storm may just be what will sooth the soul and add joy to the valley.

From the Legendary Maya Angelou

HATER

A hater is someone who is jealous and envious and spends all their time trying to make you look small so they can look tall.

They are very negative people to say the least. Nothing is ever good enough!
When you make your mark, you will always attract some haters...That's why you have to be careful with whom you share your blessings and your dreams, because some folk can't handle seeing you blessed...

It's dangerous to be like somebody else... If God wanted you to be like somebody else, He would have given you what He gave them! Right? You never know what people have gone through to get what they have...

The problem I have with haters is that they see my glory, but they don't know my story... If the grass looks greener on the other side of the fence, you can rest assured that the water bill is higher there too!
We've all got some haters among us!

People envy you because you can:
Have a **relationship with God**
Light up a room when you walk in
Start your own business
Tell a man / woman to hit the curb (if he / she isn't about the right thing)
Raise your children without both parents being in the home.
Haters can't stand to **see you happy**, Haters will never want to see **you succeed**, Haters never want you to **get the victory**, and most of our haters are people who are **supposed** to be on our side. How do you handle your **undercover** haters? You can handle these haters by:

1. **Knowing who you are and who your true friends are *(VERY IMPORTANT!!)**

2. Having a **purpose** to your life? Purpose does not mean having a job. You can have a job and still be unfulfilled. A purpose is having a **clear sense** of **what God has called you to be**. **Your purpose is not defined by what others think about you.**

3. By remembering what you have is by divine prerogative and not human manipulation.

Fulfill your dreams! You only have **one life to live**...when it's your time to leave this earth, you 'want' to be able to say, 'I've lived my life and fulfilled 'my' dreams, now I'm ready to go HOME!'

When God gives you favor, you can tell your haters, 'Don't look at me...Look at who is in charge of me...'

Watch out for Haters....................BUT most of all don't become a HATER!

I Challenge Myself

As I began to see the landscape of my life changing, I diligently sought God's direction and would keenly listen to the still small voice that was often confirmed as I went along.

Offence is a part of life, not my portion; I also know that forgiving the people who offended me is the part of life and I try to make that my portion. In my spirit, I freed myself of torment by letting go of the past injustice in order to move to higher grounds. I practiced releasing myself into the liberty of all possibilities and refused to be stagnant by fear and insecurity. In doing so, my heart began to soar to gain vision and insights to the opportunities that were before me.

I separated myself from emotional strain of the difficult circumstances that I have endured and suddenly became aware of the value of the challenges. This then confirmed to me that I have gained great wisdom and extensive insight that will benefit my fellow mankind eternally.

When I realized that the adversaries were coming against me on intimate and personal levels to accuse and condemn me, I was tempted to entertain these subtle accusation by focusing on what I thought might be my shortcomings. It was rather difficult for me to read between the lines, as the criticisms were vague. I know without a doubt God does not bring vague, indistinct correction or falsehood to anyone. This was a direct attack against me for the purpose of shutting me down so I could not fulfill my kingdom destiny; "the elimination process did not prevail"; division worked for me this time as it revealed the hidden.

I questioned the validity of the people who repeated the tales and thought of the accuracy of the information that was discussed. This was deception to its highest height and the truth is simple: deception is related to fear; according to one speaker's view of fear, "**F**alse **E**vidence **A**ppearing **R**eal." This then explained to me that even evidence can be altered and can appear to be what it is designed to be. By this time, I was slow to form judgment about the circumstances and the people as I believe it is the function of false pride to think one knows the heart and motives of an individual and form opinion based on his or her opinions. I tried my best to be generous in my evaluations by trusting folks upfront even though I was disappointed on several occasions – "grin and bear it" was not as difficult as I felt like I was growing in some areas. [1 Corinthians 2 vs. 11 – *"No one can know what anyone else is really thinking except that person alone, and no one can know God's thoughts except God's own Spirit".*

The lies that were repeated were done so as the messengers lacked knowledge, the talebearers suffered inferiority-superiority complex and some personal prejudice. Simple human relations, social conversations and behaviors were escalated and blown out of proportion by people who needed growth in different dimensions. I have learned that ignorance is like darkness; it is like being at a place where one has to feel his way out even though he has good vision, sight may be present, but he just cannot see as the element of light is absent. With ignorance, the information is available, but lack of knowledge to the facts is often the challenge. It was sad that Pam and company had to paint such picture of others to feel good about themselves. At any rate, she confessed of her jealousy and other short-comings and truly I am glad that I experienced this as I couldn't fathom this otherwise if it was told to me as it all seemed like fiction.

I separated all the extrinsic factors and asked myself, if it were another person misrepresenting and repeating the lies would I make a big deal? If the circumstances were different would the facts remain the facts? It was not worth my while to retaliate or seek refuge from unreliable sources. Thank God for the courage to forgive.

"Courage is not limited to the battlefield or bravely catching a thief in your house. The REAL tests of courage are much quieter. They are the inner tests, like remaining FAITHFUL when nobody's looking, like ENDURING pain when the room is empty, like standing ALONE when you're MISUNDERSTOOD."
Charles Swindoll

CHAPTER 4

TESTING IN THE VALLEY

TRIED ON
EVERY
SIDE; IT IS A
TEST

The word TEST came to my mind and the following acronym came with least effort; ***tried on every side; it is a test***. I asked myself on numerous occasions, why was God testing me on such levels if I was not prepared? I then recalled prior encounters and was able to compare them and found that the difference were the time and place. I was learning and gaining experiences then, which I had to apply to the present challenges. In the past, I have been victorious from similar adversaries and while I reacted differently, I knew this time I would not have to go around the mountain again if I followed the Spirit.

Verbal abuse from all types of individuals came attacking me from every angle; I was taught manners at home and it came in very handy at this time. The word *transformation* kept repeating in my heart and I accepted the fact that the refiner's fire was on me. Those insults only made me stronger and exposed the strategies of the adversary; I learnt personally that **"the bold is brawny; the coward is cruel."**

The powers of opposition were strong and persistent. I took the opportunity to re-evaluate myself and as I knew that I was in the right place spiritually and morally, I allowed God's presence to make me stronger and more persistent than the forces against me. I sometimes felt desolation approaching me and wanted to take root in my spirit, but I stood strong and the relationships with people that I once depended on for friendship and encouragement no longer provided what I needed and I was often left with a feeling of isolation. This was a hidden kind of growth that was taking place and while I was unconscious of my improvements, these were the times when I moved forward and higher with my relationship with God.

The highest result of power is often composure. The Holy Scriptures teaches that the character of Jesus of Nazareth reflects that He did not respond to the worst insults, the most mockery and ill-treatment; He remained calm and complacent with unbroken silence that might well bring resentment into the weakest heart. The strong knows the strength of being silent and to take EVERYTHING to God in prayer. Without totally conscious, I found myself practicing silence to lies, insults, provocation and found in the long run that it benefited us all.

"Father, forgive them, for they know not what they do". These were the words repeated by Jesus of

Nazareth as His own religious, unfriendly friends crucified Him; similarly, it was the people to whom I thought well of and believed in that were orchestrating the attacks in an organized and subtle strategic way. This was hard to fathom, but, in the midst of it all, I met a lady that spent most of her time in familiar settings and she was not surprised and reminded me that this type of behavior was the norm in such settings. She referenced personalities of Biblical characters in places of similarity and I became more conscious of my stand and the fact that I was improving and growing in different dimensions.

A. B. Simpson once stated, *"How much grace it requires to bear a misunderstanding rightly, and to receive an unkind judgment in holy sweetness! Nothing tests the character more than to have some evil thing said about you. This is the file that soon proves whether we are electroplated or **solid gold**. If we could only know the blessings that lie hidden in our trials we would say like David, when Shimei cursed him, "Let him curse; ... it may be ... that the Lord will be requite me good for is cursing this day."*

This is a roller-coaster, I thought, good Samaritans, kind individuals, divorce pending, car trouble that resulted in financial challenges, false rumors initiated by Pam circulating and repeated by people from all levels, mean spirited - treacherous human beings, ignorance; what next? I would ask myself. Several months of torment, turmoil, frankly "hell on earth", I would often think of my son's future, and was able to stay calm as his existence was the first thing that brought joy to me in those times. I was automatically drawn away from individuals that would contaminate my spirit as I felt the negative energy. [What a long season?] - I now know that I am not a wild plant, but a **cedar that grows on fertile ground.** I have observed that wild berries and seasonal crops grow within months of planting, but trees like cedar take years to form roots before growing into such valuable high-grade tree of the forest. The answer came as clear as day - **"LONG SUFFERING" - like it or not; it is one of the fruits of the spirit; tool for humility when being prepared for victory.**

Petty conversations that were reported one-sided and untrue became big deals to sources that I regarded in places of high standing. Drawing from prior experiences and thinking back on the manners and discipline that were instilled in me as a child came in handy. I bit my tongue and allowed it all to dissolve; the dirty remarks that were passed never really moved me, they hurt, but not to the point where I couldn't handle it.

One reason why I believe that I handled the challenges as well as I did was because realistically, humans are prune to make mistakes and while false pride teaches people to deny mistakes, I believe humility and honesty go hand-in-hand. The ego when it has the best of the human side can be very dangerous and damaging to one's self and others. The norm in almost every aspect of society is to brand one guilty until proven innocent and even today misrepresentations and false judgment brings people to prison for allegations which they are innocent of. As with the story of Joseph in the Bible; I could see myself held hostage by people who had no clue of what was happening and defended the wrong person because they lacked knowledge of the situation and even the ones who came in the middle of the mix who gathered against me without any known cause, other than the fact that they absorbed the lies and used it against me.

I would sometimes question how the things I have endured worked together for my good and I see the word humility as a mantle that must be worn and as the sign of submission to God's will. Humility also comes with a great price, for true humility is born out of adversity and complete reliance on God in such testing times. I told myself, I must face reality, *it is what it is*; per the words of 1 Kings 12:24 'This thing is from ME" ME, meaning God, the King of Kings and as Laura A. Barter Snow breaks it down:

"Have you ever thought of it, that all that concerns you concern Me too? For, "he that toucheth you, toucheth the apple of mine eye" [Zech 2:8]. You are very precious in My sight. [Isa. 43.4]. Therefore, it is My special delight to educate you. I would have you learn when temptations assail you, and the "enemy comes in like a flood," that this thing is from Me, that your weakness needs My might, and your safety lies in letting Me fight for you. Are you in difficult circumstances, surrounded by people who do not understand you, who never consult your taste, who put you in the background? This thing is from Me. I am the God of circumstances. Thou camest not to thy place by accident, it is the very place God meant for thee.

Have you not asked to be made humble? See then, I have placed you in the very school where this lesson is taught; your surroundings and companions are only working out My will. Are you in money difficulties? Is it hard to make both ends meet? This thing is from Me, for I am your purse-bearer and would have you draw from and depend upon Me. My supplies are limitless [Phil 4:19] I would have you prove my promises. Let it not be said of you, "in this thing ye did not believe the Lord your God" [Deut. 1:32]

Are you passing through a night of sorrow? This thing is from Me. I am the Man of Sorrows and acquainted with grief. I have let earthly comforters fail you, that by turning to Me you may obtain everlasting consolation [2 Thes 2:16-17]. Have you longed to do some great work for Me and instead have been laid aside on a bed of pain and weakness? This thing is from Me. I could not get your attention in your busy days and I want to teach you some of My deepest lesions. "They also serve who only stand and wait". Some of My greatest workers are those shut out from active service that they may learn to wield the weapon of all-prayer. This day I place in your hands this pot of holy oil. Make use of it free, My child. Let every circumstance that arises, every word that pains you, every interruption that would make you impatient, every revelation of your weakness be anointed with it. The sting will go as you learn to see Me in ALL THINGS".

After two weeks at Pam's house, I found a house about one mile from my son's school, where we first lived when we came into town. I signed a lease and moved in New Year's Eve. The test became more intense, as I made progress in areas of settling in a permanent job; getting situated in my new home and watching my son go off to the high school of his desire where he was excelling. At the time, I was learning on levels, versions and dimensions in life that things and people are not always who and what they **appear** to be.

My main concern was the literature I stored on my laptop; fortunately, I had some of my work saved on my Personal Computer and on discs. God, this must stop, I thought; ***"listen before you leap"*** said the still voice. I could no longer cry over spilt milk, my writings were destroyed, but I still had my brain and the desire to pursue my purpose and I felt that it was totally up to me to move on as the past is history. As I meditated on *Les Brown's* testimonies, a true motivational speaker who has impacted millions of lives and his saying, *"we must look for ways to be an active force in our own lives. We must take charge of our own destinies, design a life of substance and truly begin to live our dreams."* I believe that teaching one to take responsibility for his failures and to learn from them and improve is a good way to be productive, and in my own life, I began to make conscious efforts to be fruitful. I listened to constructive instructions, apply them to my situations and in turn have notable results.

I have accomplished many victories as I returned to graduate school to pursue my Masters in Liberal Arts as it adds value to my personal vision and allow me to improve my profession as it relates to my purpose and goals in life. I have also produced a wide variety of literature and other writings that will benefit my fellow human. I formed an organization that benefits children globally which is fulfilling and confirms that I am in my God-given element.

I decided to change my course and even evaluate intensely the people to whom I trust to associate myself with. While a man is just a man, I believe that limited people also tend to limit others. People are creatures of their environments and it is easy for one to contaminate another's field with negative energy if allowed. As with the personalities similar to Pam and the others who were used against me, I found that they all had lots in common as they were limited in experiences and exposures. They've never really absorbed anything but the familiar and I had to disconnect myself from those limited influences to avoid being stagnant.

The most joyful thing that I did was to practice releasing the offenders in the hands of God. Per the words of Jesus, *"it is impossible but that offences will come; but woe unto him, through whom they come!"* – Luke 17: 1. If verbal abuse and subduing another human is what gives one power, [*false power*] then that person is in a very sad state and I know that I cannot afford to allow people of such small minds and limited views to hinder my growth and abort my vision. As there are several routes to destinations in life, so it is that there is more than one way out of situations and I believe that the ball is in my court. As I read the following story, I was deeply convicted and searched myself to see the areas where I needed to improve as best as possible.

The Funeral

One day all the employees reached the office and they saw a big sign on the door on which read:
Yesterday, the person who has been hindering your growth in this company passed away. We invite you to join the funeral in the room that has been prepared downstairs.

In the beginning, they all got sad for the death of one of their colleagues, but after a while they started getting curious to know who was that man who hindered the growth of his colleagues and the company itself.

The excitement was such that security agents were ordered to control the crowd within the room. The more people reached the coffin, the more the excitement heated up.
Everyone thought: 'Who is this guy who was hindering my progress? Well, at least he died

One by one the thrilled employees got closer to the coffin, and when they looked inside it, they suddenly became speechless. They stood nearby the coffin, shocked and in silence, as if someone had touched the deepest part of their soul.

There was a mirror inside the coffin; everyone who looked inside it could see himself.
There was also a sign next to the mirror that read:
There is only one person who is capable of setting limits to your growth: IT IS YOU!!!!!

"There is only one person who is capable of setting limits to your growth: **IT IS YOU!** Your life does not change when your boss changes, when your friends change, when your parents change, when your husband or wife change, when your company change, when your church changes, when your location change, when your money change, when your status change...

Your life changes when YOU change, when you go beyond your limiting beliefs. Examine yourself, watch yourself. Don't be afraid of difficulties, impossibilities and losses. Be a winner; build yourself and your reality. It's the way you face Life that makes the difference!" - Unknown

I took this story personal and wondered of the areas that I needed to change and improve; I aggressively revisited some projects that I started with much enthusiasm and added to them as I was inspired to do so. I enhanced and improved my views of life by writing myself daily inspirational quotes and sending it to my email buddies across the globe. I have also developed meaningful relationships with people of vision, spend more time proactively seeking ways to better my local community and the global community at large and these activities have also brought me much fulfillment.

When I consider the Creator of the universe that His mind is full of me, ["*mindful of me*" –Psalm 8 vs. 4]. Yes! God's mind is full of me. I cannot help but be grateful and as *David Steindl-Rast* once said, "***Gratefulness*** *is the key to a happy life that we hold in our hands, because if we are not grateful, then no matter how much we have, we will not be happy -- because we will always want to have something else or something more".* While this may sound odd, even people with characters as Pam, the Pharaohs, Goliaths, and Jezebel, are in positions to sometimes bring out the best in us and reveal God's treasures, so why not be grateful for them? As the scripture says, "*pray for your enemies*", when I began to pray accordingly, that was when God revealed to me that the adversaries were truly sent by Him. While the ego may view this otherwise, a mature humble person will see that even those who ill-treat us have good ways about them; things are sometimes usually the opposite of what they *appear* to be. It may be that when a person appears to be strange and mysterious, the mystery may be perceived as a challenge to the one who lacks knowledge. According to the story of Jesus, when the traitors tried to confuse Him because He appeared strange and mysterious; He ended up confusing them. The thought that came to my mind was that non-generic brands usually out last the generic, as there is no formula to follow which is the essence of freedom to embrace the present as is; "*uphold me with thy free spirit*" – Psalm 51 v.12.

I think it was kind of Pam to invite me to her house, but it was not unusual for people to extend such kindness to me. I have allowed a lady and her daughter to live at my house at my former hometown until she got a house of her own and never charged her to stay there. I have also met others that did the same and didn't exploit the person or situation. It was the ulterior motives that were unkind and I realized it after I trusted her, I found out that she needed help for herself more than she wanted to offer help.

The Lonely Girl
Sophia Melanie Manning

*The stone which the builder refuse
I am the one they use
When they are in trouble
My energy seem to double
The Lonely Girl, yes! The Lonely Girl*

*When they are strong
They pretend that they've never done wrong
They swear and dare;
Even false witness they bare
The Lonely Girl, yes! The Lonely Girl*

*When exposed to my flaw
They remind me of the law
When I see their weakness
They tell of their meekness
The Lonely Girl, yes! The Lonely Girl*

*So much slander;
It makes me wonder
Love covers a multitude,
It brings me to the highest altitude.
The Lonely Girl, yes! The Lonely Girl*

*Eagle is who you are
Whether near or far;
Eagles sore alone
The builders always use this stone
The Lonely Girl, yes! The Lonely Girl*

*With wisdom from above,
I'll always have love
The Lonely Girl, yes! The Lonely Girl*

The Lonely Girl represents me and I would like to share this poem with the others. The person, place or thing when often used and abused by others in their weakest state seek refuge from the very same person, place or thing that have been ill-treated because of anger, bitterness, jealousy, ignorance and when the ego supersedes the divine; *the Lonely Girl is for you.* On many different levels of life, I have seen people slander others and organizations that contribute to society's well-being and before long the same slanderous tongues return to the bridge that they once crossed. The strongest people who endure adversity to the highest levels are often the ones who are called upon to help in times of trouble.

In my personal life, my mother was an educator for about forty years and I watched her rose to the level of leadership at the school where she taught for more than half of her life. She served the community with passion and did not operate as an employee of the educational system, but rather the servant who reached out to individuals and while her deeds were priceless and worth more than the benefits she received, she was hardly ever rewarded equally. I would see the same people to whom she stood up for often go against her; "*People really need help, but may attack you if you do help them; help them anyway.*" Dr. Kent M. Keith.

The Lonely Girl is not a way to encourage anyone to withdraw from community; I was as involved in community activities when I wrote this poem. I believe that God isolates us for his own plan and purpose. While pain sometimes came along with the loneliness, I was never bitter or resentful as I learned the in-depth meaning of life as it relates to my purpose, and this I can say brought the most JOY to my lonely times; my purpose is connected with my passion. The unknown writer of this excerpt explains it best:

"LET GOD ISOLATE US. In this isolating experience He develops an independence of faith and life so that the soul needs no longer the constant help, prayer, faith, or attention of his neighbor. Such assistance and inspiration from the other members are necessary and have their place in our development, but there comes a time when they act as a direct hindrance to the individual's faith and welfare. God knows how to change the circumstances in order to give us an isolating experience.

*He who flies, as an eagle does, into the higher levels where cloudless day abides, and live in the sunshine of God, must be content to live a comparatively **lonely** life. No bird is as solitary as the eagle. Eagles never fly in flocks; one, or at most two, ever being seen at once. God seeks eagle-men. No man ever comes into a realization of the best things of God, who does not, upon the God ward side of his life, learn to walk **alone** with God. Abraham **alone** in Horeb upon the heights; Moses, skilled in all the wisdom of Egypt must go forty years into the desert **alone** with God. Paul, who was filled with Greek learning and had also sat at the feet of Gamaliel, must go into Arabia and learn the desert life with God."*- Unknown

When I began to occupy my time with productivity, I forgot the challenges that I faced and encouraged myself each day that I was closer to reaching the goal. I now encourage you who experience loneliness to be productive, creative and use these times to do your own soul searching, you will find your star and hidden treasures that were birth in you by the creator of the universe. *Ramona L. Anderson* wrote a quote that has stuck with me throughout the years, "*People spend a lifetime searching for happiness; looking for peace. They chase idle dreams, addictions, religions, even other people, hoping to fill the emptiness that plagues them. The irony is the only place they ever needed to search was **within**";* I urge you to think on these words.

At a point in my life where I could use some good news and a major breakthrough, the shocking news of my dear aunt's death came and fear came sweeping over me. I was not close to anyone except Ryanne and even though I had relatives living in the city, close doesn't mean next of kin, it is more like heart-to-heart. My aunt was a goal-oriented person who was an outstanding example of someone who persevered and excelled in almost every area of her life and after being diagnosed with a terminal illness that was never heard of in our family, did not recover.

I tried to suppress my feelings, and thought I must embark on my passion and purpose in life, I have a burning desire, zeal, but, **what route must I take**? As I pictured myself in the valley and compared it to nature, valleys are usually surrounded by mountains, **"the mountain is my benchmark"** – "mountains are not to intimidate me, but to intrigue me – that is my destination", I thought and repeated to myself as I needed to encourage myself. "TRUE MOUNTAINS ARE SHAKEN ONLY BY THE CREATOR OF THE UNIVERSE". The main thing on my mind was that I have a goal to achieve and to know that it will be accomplished somehow. This thought was confirmed as I connected with words from the Holy Scriptures followed by a devotional I received from a co-worker, *"The Lord God is my strength, and he will make my feet like hinds' feet, and he will make me to walk upon mine high places" Habakkuk 3:19. – "God charts the path of His will before us. As the hinds' front feet mark the steps in which their rear feet follow, so God marks out the steps of His will before us. Our part is to place our feet in His steps. Sometimes His paths before us are steep; sometimes they are over rough and dangerous places. Yet we need not be afraid, as we place our feet securely in His steps… As God's mountaineers, we can walk on the high places of spiritual victory in Him"* - Unknown.

At this time, the logical reasoning that caught my attention was to figure out the approach to accomplish my goal and I would sometimes ask myself if I was in the right place. I didn't need to go through all of this, I have successful relatives and friends that excel in every area of life and really, I believe myself to be humble enough to call on anyone, but even though times were tough, I felt as if I was suppose to endure whatever test came my way; I knew I was in my element. The challenges of an unfamiliar environment sometimes seem unbearable, but giving up was not an option, and while I could return to my last home-town or even another city a few hours away and live closer to family, I did not believe that it was in God's plan.

Several weeks after I moved away from Pam, while preparing dinner one evening during the time of grief, Pam called and told me that she wanted to apologize of anything she cause on me, I asked her to explain what it was that she did, but she was rather vague in her response. I assured her that I held no grudges against her and I truly did not have an ounce of resentment towards her. I saw that it was necessary for an antagonist to be present in order for me to confirm that the purpose was indeed divine. The words of C. A. Fox came handy as I pondered on my emotions; *"Life's disappointments are veiled love's appointments".* I digested these words and wrote them in big letters and placed them on my night stand, so that first thing in the mornings, I would greet the day with **love's** appointments knowing that I have songs of joy in my heart and more importantly **joy** in the valley.

As time passed and Ryanne became more involved in school activities, though we lived in the school district, we were still very far from the school which made it difficult for him to balance academics and the activities. I then decided to search for a place to move closer to his school to make it more convenient. Months later, I was able to relocate to a townhouse in a neighborhood that was exactly five miles from his school. As I got situated, the roller coaster seem to start again as major challenges came facing me, why me? I asked. The answer came as I read an excerpt that was hand written in my journal. I don't quite remember where it came from, but it was rather relevant while I meditated on the moment. *"We win half the battle when we make up our minds to take the world as we find it;" – unknown.* I added including the thorns – I even wrote in all capital letters that when Paul, the Apostle asked God to remove the thorn from his flesh, God, The Almighty Himself said NO. No is an answer; it is not rejection. **NO, Not now; on-time.** I have learned to accept **NO** as a better answer than an unfaithful, untruthful or indirect yes.

Not now; On time

I Evaluate Myself

I discovered that God had provided the necessary foundation that gives assurance, stability and equilibrium and I stood stronger than ever in the face of adverse circumstances and refused to take what others say or do as personal rejection. I simply was not moved by fear or desperation, but rather by the direction and power of God; the cares that I was dealing with, God and only God was able to bring me to a place of completion, victory and honor. I had to constantly empty my heart from everything that tried to worry me, and from ego-driven, surface-based desires as they were all fatal distraction.

The tests that I faced were rather intense and I clearly saw where enemies devised schemes to create fears and disillusionment to keep me from the fulfillment of divine purpose. God extended the scepter of grace and by the power of grace I was able to overcome all that stood against me. At one point, a strange feeling came over me and I felt as though I was being disconnected from the past. This was good as separating myself from all that was behind was critical for me before I could embrace that which is ahead. My emotions got a hold of me and I had to refuse to allow these emotions to be disconcerting or to throw me into confusion. My heart was being stirred to come up higher.

I consciously made the necessary adjustments in order to conserve time, energy and resources. As I was at a critical junction in transition, I was sometimes restless and had a great desire for change, but learned that it was important that I wait and take the time to become more stable at this point rather than make any harsh decisions. I finally realized that I was in the early stages of being repositioned for greater productivity and fruitfulness. I saw where the Spirit was leading me into greater effectiveness and efficiency in all areas of my life. It was rather challenging, but I had to surrender to fine-tuning as it would ultimately make things easier and ease emotional stress.

What was this test about? Were there hidden lessons to be learned from the test that I was given?

I believe the test was simply God's way of revealing Himself to me at a higher height, the unfamiliar forces that existed and the strength that I would gain from only God when I sought his direction, trusted and moved according to His instructions. The lessons I learned were not always given in conscious states, while they were organized, they came to me as impulsive and unconscious reasoning that would later revisit my memory. When I pondered on the thoughts new revelation came about that brought me even closer to directing my entire being to God alone. The tests of life teach and prepares for the many victories ahead; Tom Bodett once said, *"the difference between school and life, in school, you're taught a lesson and then given a test. In life, you're given a test that teaches you a lesson"*.

I learned that a test is either used to evaluate a person when selected to be placed in a position, for a promotion or to prove one's ability and attitude for a particular reason. The test came from life itself and from the source of life – God. I believe it was valid as I experienced situations that cannot be explained without substantial human evidence and so the test was between me and God; revelation comes only from the Source – God.

I learned from the TEST – the bold is **brawny;** the coward is cruel; *no* is a better answer than an unfaithful, indirect yes. NO - Not now; on time. The test gave me a very good appreciation of life, humility, the valley and even the mountain. '**The mountain is my benchmark**".

The following excerpt from one of my favorite Ministers became a blue print on which I embarked on to help strengthen my faith. I have italicized the words from Dr. Schuller and wrote my personal reaction, read and re-read them as I enjoyed the "valley ride"

God Always Answers Prayer
Rev. Robert H. Schuller

When the idea is not right, God says, "NO".
No - when the idea is not the best.
No - when the idea is absolutely wrong.
No - when though it may help you, it would create problems for someone else.

I strongly believe that trusting God is accepting "***no***" as the best answer at any given time, he knows best, sees beyond the physical, controls and knows the future. All things work well, the invisible is not my portion; it is for the Almighty to decide and I take "no" as a deferred answer. A little gem I learned when I was in grade school that is still alive in me, "*good, better, best; never let it rest, until the good be better and the better, BEST.*" "No" may be good, better or sometimes the best answer one can give or take.

After a while, I made tremendous improvements in my writings and my ability to produce multiplied. I encountered unexpected challenges and disappointments related to some projects I was working on and felt that the answer "NO" was appropriate at this time as it was later revealed to me that even though my motives were sincere; the idea was not best and would have created problems for others. Giving up my rights to avoid problems for someone else, "dying to self" was my choice and it worked itself out as the plans of the adversary did not prosper.

The classic way in which I handled myself when I had to give up my rights was to encourage myself with writings from the Holy Scriptures. In Psalm 2, verses 1-4; when King David faced fierce opposition from unexpected individuals, he asked "*Why do the heathen rage and the people imagine a vain thing? The kings of the earth set themselves, and the rulers take counsel together, against the Lord, and against His anointed, saying, Let us break their bands asunder, and cast away their cords from us*".

David confirms that God is still in control when in the fourth verse he declares, *"He [God] that sitteth in the heavens shall laugh: the Lord shall have them in derision."*

When the time is not right, God says, "SLOW".
What a catastrophe it would be if God answered every prayer at the snap of your fingers. Do you know what would happen? God would become your servant, not your master. Suddenly God would be working for you instead of you working for God.

The race is not for the swift, nor the battle for the strong;" ENDURANCE" was the word I chose to stand on. As I stood face-to-face with situations and possibilities that I could never have imagined, my inclination was to make decisions based on how I felt, but that was not my best recourse; I became more patient and took time to seek God for wisdom and guidance. I had to exercise my faith and watch it grow exceedingly as God is the Author and Finisher of my faith. This was an **extreme** moment and I knew that what God had written over me was coming to pass. A new chapter of **extreme faith** was written over me as it was necessary to meet and overcome **extreme challenges.**

The word "*SLOW*" reminds me of driving and observing the sign that alerts us to be slow; "the slow sign sometimes cautions us of unseen hazards ahead and if we obey or disobey there are also unseen results and consequences. Even with natural disasters, a storm for example usually slows us down from our normal speed, but it doesn't stop us. Slow sometimes even mean that we are being taught a lesson that requires our undivided attention so we won't fail the next time around. Slow is now one of the signs that I have observed and purpose to obey as this is when I can truly hear from God clearly without distraction.

> *When you are not right, God says, "GROW."*
> *The selfish person has to grow in unselfishness.*
> *The cautious person must grow in courage.*
> *The timid person must grow in confidence;*
> *The dominating person must grow in sensitivity.*
> *The critical person must grow in tolerance.*
> *The negative person must grow in positive attitudes.*
> *The pleasure-seeking person must grow in compassion for suffering people.*

Growth is essential to life; it hinders stagnancy, broaden horizons and gives desire to explore the beauty of creation. For the fruits of the Spirit to be seen, growth is vital; *love, joy*, and *peace* doesn't come about like the wind, it is contrary situations and circumstances that proves the presence of these fruits. Jacob and others were sometimes unlovable, but I had to allow the Spirit in me to rise above the mistake I made and kept moving. During growth, I learnt reality at its best; I was pruned and developed a more conscious way of approaching the things that produce substantial results in my life and the lives of others. My courage to pursue my dreams grew and I became more patient and tolerant of aggressive situations. The best course of action was to withdraw from pressures momentarily, rise up in the Spirit, seek God's guidance and ask for wisdom. I had to bring myself to a place of peace in my soul so that I could be led by God alone, as to do otherwise would only create more chaos and confusion.

> *When everything is all right, God says, "GO."*
> *Then miracles happen:*
> *A hopeless alcoholic is set free.*
> *A drug addict finds release.*
> *A doubter becomes a child in his belief.*
> *Diseased tissue responds to treatment, and healing begins.*
> *The door to your dream suddenly swings open and there stands God saying, "GO!"*
> *Remember: God's delays are not God's denials.*
> *God's timing is perfect.*
> *Patience is what we need in prayer.*

The answer "GO" came to me like the green light at a traffic light; it signaled me when to take off in the right direction, the right time and place. "GO" came at various moments with least effort; when there was time for a change of scene and for me to take that leap of faith to launch the non-profit organization, return to graduate school and embrace a new set of social associates; without question, divine alignment and connections were at hand – "GO". At this time, I didn't need to justify or reason the logic of my purpose, but I declared my intent to myself and the written plan and desire for manifestation came without force; joy, fulfillment and complete freedom was my portion. *"It is the blessing of the Lord that maketh rich and He adds "no" sorrow to it*; Proverbs 10 vs. 22.

As time passed and my son began to mature and became responsible, self-sufficient, independent, and of age to work, he spent one summer holiday volunteering at the local library, serving the community and gaining experience and exposure to community actions. The summer holidays after, he worked amongst medical professionals in different areas of practice and was able to help himself financially. The "GO" time was a time of abundance in my spirit and in the manifestation of God's promises and I heard directly from God through the results that came about. I then began to look for opportunities to grow the non-profit organization and developed meaningful relationships with people of vision and purpose; partner with and contribute to the different local and global projects. Humility; even when the results of the test proved me worthy, I knew I must continue to walk in humility, to be called a winner.

Reverend Schuller, you are indeed a legend and I personally thank you for being such an inspirational forerunner that has added "*joy to my valley*" through this excerpt. This intriguing litany has compelled me to compose a personal assignment which is an exercise I used to evaluate my progress and these words were the point of reference I chose which brought forth conviction and consolation simultaneously that kept me in a balanced state. From the valley where much joy was experienced; I salute you!

"Character cannot be developed in ease and quiet. Only through experience of trial and suffering can the soul be strengthened, ambition inspired, and success achieved." Helen Keller

CHAPTER 5

FACING THE VALLEY

I truly believe the words of Romans 8 vs. 28 & 29 –
"*God causes everything to work together for the good of those who love God and are called according to his purpose for them. For God knew His people in advance, and he chose them.*"

One great reality is that memories don't live like people do. Unless a person suffers from Alzheimer disease, he will always remember excited times and adverse situations; we often hear examples during sermons, messages or interviews of personal experiences that live on. The soul is a bundle of memories and the center of one's emotions; when I see things for what they are, it is easier for me to forgive. When I see things the way I would like them to be, it is more difficult, it's like reality and consciousness verses fantasy. "**Denial is dangerous.**"

In addition to the many adversities that involved individuals, I got hit with negative ratings on my credit report which all resulted from my divorce. I prematurely left graduate school and the student loans were reported as negative instead of deferred. Again human error caused me to be judged as there were those who used my credit report as means of evaluating me without knowing the truth of my circumstances. There was also identity theft and other people were reporting income under my name which became another major burden when I discovered it and I had to hire an attorney that handled tax issues to conduct the investigation which added more to my expenses. Thank God, within three months of corresponding with the taxing authorities, I was released from all the counts against me.

One disaster after another was what I dealt with over an extended period, yet in the depth of my heart there was still the desire and longing to keep the spiritual connection with God. The *still small voice* would remind me that He had not left me and loves me unconditionally. I would encourage myself as I knew that God saw, knew and understood my plight and I had come too far to abort the vision in me.

Negative thoughts came about when the misrepresentation and conspiracy were forming but I pressed through the thoughts that tried to hinder and obscure my emotional healing; thoughts of fear, doubt and unbelief. My portion at this time was to rise up in my new potential in the anointing that God decreed for me; the purpose He had for my life.

"*Joy comes in the morning*". A while later, after all I went through, I received an email from the pastor at the church I last attended and his words to me were that Jacob came to the church and cried at the altar all throughout the service. Jacob also confessed that he was communicating with a priest that worshipped contrary to my spiritual beliefs. This was shocking to me, but I thought that if he confessed, it was good for us both, as I needed to know where the trouble started. I had served children in various organizations and while waiting for a reference to volunteer at a local organization, I got an encouraging word through email from the children's pastor as she had provided an excellent reference for me. I had recently met and gave a co-worker a ride in her time of car trouble and she offered me to add her as a reference when she heard me telling my friend that I was skeptical as to who I wanted to know my business at that stage. This was good as I was still suffering a little shame and reproach and needed one other person to add as a personal reference for a local volunteer application that I was completing.

When I felt the despairing thoughts returning, I shifted my focus to making things work out, "*this too shall pass*", I would often repeat out loud and write in bold letters. The obstacles then became opportunities for hope rather than increasing to an attribute of despair. I tried my best to ignore the negative things that I was facing as I was developing a social relationship with a couple who my son and I met at a community outreach. They appeared to be good-natured and were involved in community organizations that involved teenagers and initiated kindness to my son. The lady took Ryanne and some other children to a mid-week youth group. We then developed a social relationship as I transported the children to their home as we lived in the same neighborhood. In the times when I experienced car issues, the couple loaned me one of their vehicles and as I progressed in one area, other challenges would show up from different directions.

I would often question why is it that this season seemed so prolonged and my faith would be exhausted of waiting for this period to end. One day while experiencing a quiet moment and meditating on the following excerpt, the reason for the fruit "long suffering" was confirmed:

The secret of the Lord is with them that fear him [Ps. 25:14]. *There are secrets of providence which God's dear children may learn. His dealings with them often seem, to the outward eye, dark and terrible. Faith looks deeper and says, "This is God's secret." You look only on the outside; I can look deeper and see the hidden meaning." Sometimes diamonds are done up in rough packages, so that their value cannot be seen. When the tabernacle was built in the wilderness there was nothing rich in its outside appearance. The costly things were all within, and its outward covering of rough badger skin gave no hint of the valuable things which it contained".*

"God may send you, dear friends, some costly packages. Do not worry if they are done up in rough wrappings. You may be sure there are treasures of love, and kindness, and wisdom hidden within. If we take what He sends, **and trust Him** *for the goodness in it, even in the dark, we shall learn the meaning of the secrets in providence."* A.B. Simpson

"I am on the right track," I told myself, I couldn't help but laugh at how the puzzle was being solved, manifestation was now visible; I had to keep my feet on the ground and not allow the subtle lethal spirit of false pride to creep in. I came across this poem and thought, "*how comforting?*" this is a keeper and the words are good to remember when in the valley as I knew that I was being prepared to soar with the eagles on the mountain top:

> *Always Remember God gives you.....*
> *Enough Happiness to keep you Sweet*
> *Enough Trials to keep you Strong*
> *Enough Sorrows to keep you Human*
> *Enough Hope to keep you Happy*
> *Enough Failure to keep you Humble*
> *Enough Success to keep you Eager*
> *Enough Friends to give you Comfort*
> *Enough Wealth to meet your Needs*
> *Enough Enthusiasm to make you look forward*
> *Enough Faith to banish depression, and*
> *Enough Determination to make each day a better day than the last.* – Elham Binai

Reality

Staying in touch with me was not very hard, as I consider myself spirit-based and God-fearing; truly, these challenges brought me closer to the divinity. I didn't connect to anyone as I knew what true friendships are and I just didn't find mature and trust worthy people.

While making attempts to proceed with some projects that I was working on, I reverted to an old journal and came across the following excerpt that I first learned of when I attended a retreat at the beautiful Smoky Mountains in Tennessee: *"Those who have had many dealings with God know well the value of secret fellowship with Him, to ascertain His will. Are you in difficulty about your way? Go to God with your question; get the direction from the light of His smile or the cloud of His refusal."*

Taken from the journal of George Fox.
It took a long while for me to digest all the happenings around me as things were moving at such fast speed. Again, things seemed to be repeating and a series of events were multiplying, but with a clear conscience, I know that I did not initiate any ill-will, neither am I ever about trouble so I didn't allow it to bother me. I am not the enemy, and if the offender is believed to be the winner of the game; there is always the championship. The initial offense gives reason for defense and as they say in the ball game, "*offense wins game; defense wins championship*". The offenses that were brought on me from the inception of the valley season and with direction from God and my ability to use love, forgiveness and productivity as my defense brought about growth and advanced spiritual insights.

Ignatius once said, "*God has made me bread for His elect, and if it be needful that the bread must be ground in the teeth of the lion to feed His children, blessed be the name of the Lord.*"

A great pioneer of the mission field of all times, Mrs. Charles E. Cowman wrote "*poverty, hardship and misfortune have pressed many a life to moral heroism and spiritual greatness. Difficulty challenges energy and perseverance. It calls into activity the strongest qualities of the soul. It was the weights on father's old clock that kept it going. Many a headwind has been utilized to make port. God has appointed opposition as an incentive to* **faith and holy activity***.*

The most illustrious characters of the Bible were bruised and threshed and ground into bread for the hungry. Abraham's diploma styles him as "the father of the faithful". That was because he stood at the head of his class in affliction and obedience. *"Jacob suffered severe thrashings and grindings. Joseph was bruised and beaten and had to go through Potiphar's kitchen and Egypt's prison to get to his throne.*

"David, haunted like a partridge on the mountain, bruised, weary and footsore, was ground into bread for a kingdom. Paul never could have been bread for Caesar's household if he had not endured the bruising, whippings and stoning. He was ground into fine flour for the royal family".

How about a little humor in the midst of this terror? I must free myself from emotional distress, I thought, and so, to add humor to my current condition and in making fun of the adversaries and their schemes, I thought of the processing of fruit juices and compared myself as being processed like a "*smoothie drink.*" This is a drink composed of different kinds of fruits, chopped, mixed, blended and whipped in the blender or juicer and when completed is mild and nutritious and is enjoyed by fruit lovers like me. The results of the various attacks didn't show a trace of the bruises, but I ended up better than I started. Just as the different fruits cannot be identified individually, so it is with me, no trace of the heartaches are visible; if it were not for the written public record of the divorce and the other adversities, one could not tell of the attacks. The poisonous lies and dirty remarks did not have much adverse effect on me as intended.

"Power is developed by resistance. The way electricity is produced in the powerhouse yonder is by the sharp friction of the revolving wheels. And so we shall find some day that even Satan has been one of God's agencies of blessings" – from **Days of Heaven upon Earth."**

I had to face the facts as facts; I just couldn't connect with a sincere friend to bond with long-term regardless of the efforts I placed on social relationships. I was almost always faced with opposition, jealousy and treacherous back-stabbers; all of whom were feeding from the damage that Pam did to me without knowing the root of their actions and they even added their own versions. In one sense, I believed that I limited myself to a narrow group when I could have explored the community at large. I am a social butterfly and have never been conformed to any particular group so I decided later to seek ways to be involved with other community groups. I had no ill-feeling towards anyone, and for *my own soul's sake*, I chose to practically educate myself on **forgiveness.**

What is forgiveness: Forgiveness according to Robert D. Heidler is defined as *"an act of the will in which we choose to give up our right to hold another person accountable for the wrong they have done us"*. *"It is releasing the person who harmed you."* **Robert goes on further to say,** *"when we refuse to forgive, we are attempting to "hold on" to the person who hurt us. We feel that by holding them we can somehow make them pay and "settle the score". In reality, all we are doing is harming ourselves by letting our hearts become filled with bitterness and anger. Un-forgiveness does not harm the other person."*

I also agree with Robert's views that *"forgiveness is not **denying** the offense, it is the **choice** to **release** that person and when we do so, we are free to move forward."* In my many encounters with people from all walks of life, I have never met a person who held grudges to be sincere in their endeavors or willing to celebrate others; they often seem to take out their frustrations on people who seem to be happy and carefree. It usually doesn't take long to figure out that the person struggles with un-forgiveness. On the other hand, a jovial person is usually proactive and offers assistance **without reservations;** is usually forgiving almost all the time and have good experiences to share.

When it comes to un-forgiveness, the people who rebel and are always retaliating and responding to suite the ego and image are usually easy for me to win. I use David's words of Psalm 68:6, "**God sets the solitary in families: he brings out those which are bound with chains: but the rebellious dwell in a dry land.**" With forgiveness, I am better able to appreciate the advantage of the present, as in order for me to survive; I must always release myself from past burdens to allow the process of change to form in me. I must also rid myself from the harm of old memories and realize that the rebirth comes after forgiving the offenses.

"Some people get easily turned aside from the grandeur of their life-work by pursuing their own grievances and enemies, until their life gets turned into one little petty whirl of warfare. It is like a nest of hornets. You may disperse the hornets, but you will probably get terribly stung, and get nothing for your pains, for even their honey is not worth a search." A.B. Simpson

The Pruning Period

The real test was to yield to the process of nurturing as I was being refined and pruned so that I could represent love in every aspect, and so I had no choice but to allow the process to occur. I knew I had waste material that needed to be discarded and I also knew that I would have to make the ultimate decision to be practical in my living in order to move forward. After I discovered the behavior patterns of people who were limited in their experiences and their views of life, I avoided close relationships with them. I continued in searching myself to adapt and adjust to situations accordingly, even though I was resilient in the stands I took. I felt as if I improved in many areas including spending time and developing a closer parent relationship with my son.

Through reading literature from some of the world's greatest writers and applying some of the suggested proven solutions, I have decided to design a substantial path to begin to live my dream. Let me share the following excerpt that was handed to me by a co-worker one day as I sat in the lunchroom enjoying a spinach salad:

*"**God** has a **life pattern** for us and begins to fit it to the fabric of our lives. Some **rearranging** may be **necessary** to make the **pattern fit**. Some **attitudes**, **desires,** or **motives** may have to be **adjusted**. As He begins to cut the fabric, **some things will require cutting out completely**. Other things will only need **trimming**. This process may **hurt**, but it is **necessary** in order to **complete** the garment for **His good pleasure** ... **God adds finishing touches to bring out His beauty in our lives. No***

two lives are designed alike; He has **His own special pattern for each** of us." Unknown. *"It is God which worketh in you both to will and to do of his good pleasure"* [Philippians 2:13]

I must admit that pruning and purging were essential in order for me to have the victory. The processing and transition were not comfortable, but my view of the season was that the unseen force of the universe is in control and my heart was not troubled as my mind was fixed on the expected results. Even then, from time to time, the past would come to my spirit in a hurting way as if I was in the wrong, and flashbacks of where I had been, what I had done, my failures and misfortunes, and even how others had failed me. Before going in a state of self-pity, I would be sure to give the enemy credit for his ploy to overwhelm me with sadness and grief in order to obliterate my joy, but would also realized that this is a distraction from God's will and purpose for my life. I continually practiced to use those times to forgive and release the past so that I would be free to manifest and express the fruit of the Spirit.

John 15:2 *"And every branch that beareth fruit he purgeth it, that it may bring forth more fruit"*

- The story told by Homera Homer-Dixon; *a child of God was dazed by the variety of afflictions which seemed to make her their target. Walking past a vineyard in the rich autumnal glow she noticed the untrimmed appearance and the luxuriant wealth of leaves on the vines, that the ground was given over to a tangle of weeds and grass, and that the whole place looked utterly uncared for; and she pondered, the* heavenly Gardener whispered so precious a message that she would fain pass it on.

My dear child, are you wondering at the sequence of trials in your life? **Behold** the vineyard and **learn of it**. The gardener ceases to prune, to trim, to harrow, or to pluck the ripe fruit only when he expects nothing more from the vine during that season. It is left to itself, because that the season of fruit is past and further effort for the present would yield no profit. Comparative uselessness is the condition of freedom from suffering. Do you then wish me to cease pruning your life? Shall I leave you alone? And the comforted heart cried, "No!"

FOR MY OWN SOUL'S SAKE
I OFTEN REPEATED THIS PRAYER –
Selected verses from Faith Dube

    Father
Let every wound of my past dissolve in the light of Your wonderful presence. Turn my weaknesses into strengths, my failures into victories, my sorrows into joy. Perfect all that concerns me.

    Father,
Your kingdom of love is in my heart.
It is not I who live but Christ who lives
in me. Your kingdom is established in my
spirit. Your kingdom has come into my emotions,
and they are in a healthy balance.
Your kingdom has come into my mind,
and it is sanctified. Your kingdom
has come into my body, and I am becoming
healthy. Your kingdom rules my heart, and
I live a life of richness and depth. Your
kingdom has come into my mouth, and I speak
words that heal and liberate. Because Your
kingdom rules my life I am resilient and
filled with hope in all circumstances.

Father,
You have always taken care of me, and
You always will. You give me what
I need each day and prepare for my
tomorrow. My faith is growing. Thank
You for my daily joy that draws me
to worship when sadness comes. Thank
You for Your healing balm that soothes
the day's aches and pains. Thank
You for Your perfect love that soaks
away my fear. Your tender daily
care in every area of need draws me
to my knees in worship. Thank You
for walking with me day by day.
In our growing friendship You have
never failed me, ever. I love You,
Father.

Father,
Thank You for Your gift of mercy in my life;
Your mercy that reaches my heart, because I have
forgiven those who hurt me. I confess my sins and
receive forgiveness. I am free from condemnation
and safely united to You. Your truth has made me free.
I love You Father.

Father,
By your grace I let go of
bitterness resentment and un-forgiveness.
If there are hidden roots of un-forgiveness,
thank You for shining Your light on them.
I entrust this area to You. Thank You, for
turning injury into compassion and hurts
into intercessions. Forgiveness brings
heaven to earth. I love You, Father

Father,
Thank You for protecting me from every evil and for
bringing me a gift of peace. You have broken the chain
of oppression, delivered me from depression, anger, guilt, and

*fear. I cast down every argument and every
high thing in me that exalts itself against the
knowledge of God. Thank You for giving me
the power over all the power of the enemy. Nothing
shall hurt me. Thank You for Your armor, Your name,
Your Spirit. No weapon formed against me shall prosper.
Thank You Father. I love You.*

    Father,
Every gift You have given me, every dream, every talent, every possession, every resource and hope for the future, I return to You with love. All is Yours. May Your name be glorified, may Your kingdom come Take Lord, receive, All my liberty, My memory, my understanding, my entire will. All that I have and possess, You have given all to me; To You, O' Lord, I return it. All is Yours. Dispose of it wholly according to Your will. Give me Your love and Your grace, for this is sufficient for me. Amen!!

My soul is my treasure and I must guard it from being contaminated with energy from the wrong force or source, and so, repeating the above-referenced prayer became a habit that kept me moving which resulted in abounding joy and freedom.

Revelation
TIME
IS THE
MASTER OF
EVERY THING

As I became sensitive to the Spirit of God, listened and yielded to His leading, God began to reveal things that were hidden. At this time what had been obscured in darkness and even designed for my destruction came out as plain as day. What I discovered provided crucial information that helped me choose a course of action for the steps I would need to take.

Dr. Jowett once said *"when God delays, He is not inactive. He is getting ready His instruments, He is ripening our powers; and at the appointed moment we shall arise equal to our task. Even Jesus was 30 years in privacy, growing in wisdom before He began His work". God is never in a hurry but spends years with those He expects to greatly use. He never thinks the days of preparation too long or too dull. The hardest ingredient in suffering is often TIME. He shall sit as a refiner and purifier of silver, but He knows how long, and like a true goldsmith He stops the fires the moment He sees His image in the glowing metal.*

We may not see now the outcome of the beautiful plan which God is hiding in the shadow of His hand; it yet may be long concealed; but faith may be sure that He is sitting on the throne, calmly waiting the hour when, with adoring rapture, we shall say, "all things have worked together for good". Like Joseph, let us be more careful to learn all the lessons in the school of sorrow than we are anxious for the hour of deliverance. There is a "need-be" for every lesion, and when we are ready, our deliverance will surely come, and we shall find that we could not have stood in our place of higher service without the very things that were taught us in the ordeal. God is educating us for the future, for higher service and nobler blessings; and we have the qualities that fit us for a throne, nothing can keep us from it when God's time has come. Don't steal tomorrow out of God's hands. Give God time to speak to you and reveal His will. He is never too late; learn to wait".

During the threat of a storm while preparing to evacuate to my relatives in a city about three hours away, my car overheated and the engine was damaged. The following week at a volunteer gathering, before servicing at the team meeting, the leader of the group as usual asked for prayer requests, I mentioned my car situation. A day or two later, I picked up my phone to call a friend for a referral for a mechanic and mistakenly dialed one of the volunteers on the team. She mentioned to me that I was on her heart and it was not a co-incidence that I called her. She asked if my car was fixed and I explained to her that the engine was damaged. She became concerned about my being able to replace a car engine and in concluding the phone conversation she asked me to hold the line as she would discuss with her husband about helping me. When she came back on the phone line, she offered to pay the full cost of the car repair. This was a tangible miracle that showed that prayers are always answered by God in His time and how He chooses.

While my car was being repaired, I had to rent a car as my neighborhood does not provide public transportation. Upon returning the rental car, as I entered the building to process the return on the rental, I was greeted by the host of the community festival that I attended when I was new in town. On the last day when Pam and I attended, she met Pam and exchanged information without my knowledge. I completely placed Pam and the incidents behind me as I had already overcame other challenges. She didn't hesitate to tell me what Pam told her and suddenly, I remembered the series of conversations and encounters with others, which then confirmed to me that unkind words were aimed at me in Pam's defense from sources that were not knowledgeable of the truth. I was not moved, but clearly remembered events of subtle, indirect confrontations from unfriendly friends that corresponded information to other sources. In any event, the good news for that day was that I got confirmed information of the enmity that was developed against me without cause and better yet selected by the rental car company for a waiver on my rental and paid only taxes for the week's rental. How mysterious this was, I thought, it didn't cost me anything to fix my car or to get the rental car, but the confirmed information that was given by the lady only gave me courage to press on.

I had flashbacks of events that occurred with people who I thought were kind to me upfront but realized how treacherous they were as it was later revealed that they were all monitored and coached to extract information to provoke me without knowing the reason for their own acts. What they did not know was that I was ahead in the game and I had to play along to test the sincerity to their self-righteous remarks. I could only image how amazing the conscience can haunt a person when it suffers guilt and I wished that they could see my heart as while they were using their heads to imagine mischief, I was using my heart to forgive them. I am not playing the perfectionist card, but I had to wonder to myself, what was this about, when in fact this was petty compared to the real issues that required substantial effort to endure.

When I thought about the situation, I could have repeated some of the unkind statements and argued the points on several occasions and even proved the methods as unreliable and invalid. I have learned from prior experience to this particular time that "it makes no sense to argue with cruel people as they will bring you down to their level of cruelty and *seemingly* win you with their formulated experiences." I would often consider the methods that were used to test me and I pondered on the **validity** and the **reliability** that didn't seem to have substantial reasoning. A leader once said, *"sometimes it is better to play your own devil's advocate and stand on the front-line; this way you get the results first-handed."* The choice was mine and "*instant forgiveness*" became my logo and with ease, I gladly released them - **"where there is injury; pardon"** – St. Francis of Assisi

A great Brazilian writer, Paulo Coelho stated *"We can never judge the lives of others, because each person knows only their own pain and renunciation. It's one thing to feel that you are on the right path, but it's another to think that yours is the only path."* I remembered Pam sharing with me that she was raised by parents who didn't show attention and she was exposed to real life from her early pre-teenage years. I thought, maybe she is truly hurting and the best she could do is find an outlet, and I might be the most vulnerable. But again, I asked, why? Was I tested, missing the point, or being exposed to the real deal to its fullest, *'where there is darkness; light"* – **St. Francis of Assisi.**

I had a choice to either let things be, or play the same game; *"tit for tat"* – how trifling? I thought. It then occurred to me that this had to be about a major circumcision and transition. Whatever it was, in one sense, had the best of me and in the next I had the best of it as it made me stronger and taught me the test of life as well as the lessons that went along with them. Gossip and untrue tales were told before me, about people from all walks of life, including some of the most significant, so I thought this season is for a higher purpose and kept on going.

 It was rather difficult for me to even imagine individuals who had to paint negative pictures of others to feel good about themselves; or, to be accepted among certain groups, while they and some of their own were suffering from all kinds of issues and identity complexes. I can do better than that, I thought to myself as I had my own shortcomings and challenges that I was trying to work on and I aimed at living a life of victory. *'Where there is hatred; let me sow love"* – ***St. Francis of Assisi***

I Evaluate Myself

I experienced God lifting me beyond my circumstances and trials and gave me victory over everything the enemy brought against me. It was my duty to arise and let power of the anointing of destiny flow, climb the mountain of the creator where the water is fresh and the rivers flow in the power of truth and revelation; I then decided to walk no more in the low land. When I asked diligently of God to show me ways to overcome the problems I faced, the first answer I got was *"rise above my feelings of oppression and sense of being a victim, in order to truly receive wisdom"*.

A new level of hope and faith was imparted in me and as I took heed to the presence of God surrounding me, I realized that was what I needed to carry me through the next leg of the journey ahead of me. I connected my spirit with the Holy Spirit and fed daily on this mighty impartation, soaked in this conveyance as I journeyed through and allowed God to transport me to a higher position of confidence and trust.

I gained a greater understanding of my authority by further defining my responsibilities. I realized that this was something that needed to be brought into divine order before God would promote me with additional duties. Submission to God's ultimate authority was imperative and humility was the order in which I operated, as I believed that God's authority had nothing to do with pride and superiority. Upon surrendering all, I experienced a sense of power that manifested in proportion to the measure of my submission to God. I recognized an undefined restlessness and a desire for new vibrancy and fresh anointing. God was calling me out of a place of stagnation by causing me to stir up the gift that is within me and the afflictions that I endured were working for me far more exceeding than against me.

Was I conscious of my surroundings? Was I aware of the pruning period and the results it brought forth?

Yes, at least seventy-five percent of the time I was aware of the opportunists and the vultures that would interrupt and contaminate any progressive efforts in order to fit in with the crowd. Some were lethal rattlesnakes and it was extremely hard to discern who the enemy was at all times. [*"you catch a rattle snake, by being a better rattlesnake"* – **Mississippi Burning**]. I was not exposed to friends of such nature at this level and this close, so it was rather hard for me to fathom that this type of behavior was real.

I believe it should always be an honor to serve others that are in need. I recall at a casual event, a speaker once referenced that a person went down to "the level of another to assist." I thought these folks have it backwards as I believe that it should be considered a privilege to offer help to others in whatever circumstances and be glad that they are blessed to be a blessing. Those words were contrary to life and the meaning of true life, but in any event, I was aware of the pruning and would not dear think of myself as inferior or superior to anyone else no matter what.

I believe people help others because they want to help; I also believe people who speak with such false power premeditate on hurting others and do so because they intend to hurt to suit their ego. One of the most disappointing observations I made was that people seemed to be fulfilled when they hurt other people's feelings, but were not able to even face their own failures or short comings until conviction returns to haunt them. This behavior type was rather immature and I had to keep strong as I went along.

I was conscious of the problem and that the lethal spirit of pride was at work and so, I had to be humble in my approach and responses as I interacted with people. The greatest result from the pruning period was to know that I truly forgave even the giants. While adjusting and adapting to situations as they came, I became more resilient in standing and making better decisions.

GROWING AND GAINING WISDOM THROUGH AWARNESS AND OBSERVING CONSCIOUS LIVING BRINGS "JOY" IN THE VALLEY

CHAPTER 6

JOY IN THE VALLEY

For each new morning with its light,
For rest and shelter of the night,
For health and food, for love and friends,
For everything Thy goodness sends.
For flowers that bloom about our feet;
For tender grass, so fresh, so sweet;
For song of bird, and hum of bee;
For all things fair we hear or see,
Father in heaven, we thank Thee! ~Ralph Emerson

I would often repeat the above-referenced verse and took an objective, optimistic view on life as the days came. I practiced ignoring the negativity of the past as I would see it as spilt milk. It was gone. I was not hoping for a troubled future and so, I did not worry my mind with negative energy, I learned to live in the present and made it so beautiful that it will be worth remembering.

As I meditated on current conditions, I became aware that I was indeed making steady progress in solving long-term problems. The process included a realignment of elements on my physical, emotional, mental and spiritual levels. I gained greater spiritual clarity and insight. I became conscious that I was emerging from a rather lengthy and troubling period of relative uncertainty and I took full advantage. One cannot take the logic out of life; "*whatsoever things are true*". As I completely released myself from all words spoken in anger, bitterness, and resentment, even then, I still faced a prolonged negative group that suffered low self-esteem, insecurity and identity complexes. I took this time to deal with and correct long-term problems as I had the courage and insight to look squarely at every situation and make decisions that were long overdue.

While facing the facts of life, I had to purposely choose to be in a state of happiness, as I believe that it is the inner me that generate happiness and I could not look for it to come from another person, situation or place. One legendary writer once defined happiness as "*that which we think and feel and do, first for the other fellow and then for ourselves.*" – Unknown

> *Kindness in **words** creates **confidence**.*
> *Kindness in **thinking** creates **profundity**.*
> *Kindness in **giving** creates **LOVE**.* – Lao Tzu

I am in agreement with this short verse by Tzu. I also believe that one cannot be in a joyful state if he purposely subdues others with mean words, thoughts and deeds; it is usually the struggle to be recognized as superior that breeds those types of behaviors which are often revealed in time. One cannot become the *instrument of peace* unless there is turmoil to combat with love; such as the constant uproar of gossip and lies. There would be no need for me to sow *love* and *pardon* if ill-words and deeds were not uttered out of bitterness, anger, arrogance and false pride. I would not have been able to relate to someone who needs *consolation* and *understanding*, if I've never experienced this trauma in this time of my life. I now realized the connection of the prayer of St. Francis that I prayed several years ago and its relevance to my personal relationship with God and man; '**all of the above matters"** and is sometimes the best answer to guess.

Nature teaches of seasons; Spring, Summer, Autumn and Winter, during these seasons, the atmosphere, climatic conditions and temperature changes. It can be seen as the vegetation and trees show different colors and growth stages; even the rising and setting of the sun changes along with the times. I have had the privilege to live in different geographic areas and have experienced the four distinct seasons where I had to be prepared to dress for the weather accordingly. This was one way how I absorbed the story of the Heartsease as it explains my reason for being strong, resilient and optimistic through the roller coaster ride in the valley.

The story of the Heartease goes like this, *"the king of a village went into his garden one morning, and found everything withered and dying. He asked the oak that stood near the gate what the trouble was. He found it was sick of life and determined to die because it was not tall and beautiful like the pine. The pine was all out of heart because it could not bear grapes, like the vine. The vine was going to throw its life away because it could not stand erect and have as fine a fruit as the peach tree. The geranium was fretting because it was not tall and fragrant like the lilac; and so all through the garden. Coming to a heartease, he found its bright face lifted as cheery as ever. "Well, heartease, I'm glad, amidst all this discouragement, to find one brave little flower. You do not seem to be the least disheartened. "No, I am not of much account, but I thought that if you wanted an oak, or a pine, or a peach tree, or a lilac, you would have planted one; but as I knew you wanted a heartease, I am determined to be the best little heartease that I can."* Excerpt from Annie Johnson Flint.

I found myself emulating the heartese and hereby beseech you to do the same; set your heart at ease with everyone who set himself against you without any logical cause, he cannot get the victory over you. When one's destiny is connected to the best that life has to offer, he strip himself of everything and in this nakedness find all things restored one hundred fold. **"DESTINY IS DIVINE"**.

Our perception must be of true reasoning and to know that God protects us for His own purposes; we must therefore look for the brighter side, or even the unknown as it is full of great possibilities. As observed throughout the ages, when there is value in any type of resource, the processing period is rather intense and is known by the processor. With me, the significance of my purpose had to be birth out of adverse circumstances as I was carefree when I knew that I was supposed to be more careful and I strongly believe that God had to use the rod of correction to get my attention. The discovery of Jacob's deception, all the insulting words that were aimed to hurt my feelings, the painful news, the cruel wound of the unfriendly friends, betrayals and financial difficulties – God knows and is still in control. I have had an advance course in practicing to trust and obey the creator of the universe more and more and even more.

One lesson I learned in the valley was the value of being truly broken, which I believe is a treasure in of itself. Line upon line, precept by precept, I have seen the favor from the Creator in countless ways that were rather mysterious. *"God never uses anybody to a large degree, until after He breaks that one all to pieces. Joseph had more sorrow than all the other sons of Jacob and it led him out into a ministry of bread for all nations. For this reason, the Holy Spirit said of him, "Joseph is a **fruitful** bough … by a well, whose branches run over the wall" Gen 49:22. It takes sorrow to widen the soul* "- From the Heavenly Life".

When I least expected, one Thanksgiving holiday a lady who I met and developed a social relationship with called and offered Ryanne a car. This was the gift of his lifetime as he was saving and hoping to buy a car in the near future. The car was in excellent driving condition and was worth a market value of a new car. I made a point to celebrate with Ryanne and advised him to give God all the glory as this was a tangible way to explain answered prayers. As the writer of this excerpt explain: *"God does not open paths for us in advance of our coming. He does not promise help before help is needed. He does not remove obstacles out of our way before we reach them. Yet when we are on the edge of our need, God's hand is stretched out. You will not have "dying grace" when you are in good health."* J.R.M.

I have proven numerous times that when I allow nature to take its course, the results are much better than inducing effort. When I was doubtful and impatient, I bore enough consequences to realize the truth. The legendary H.C. Trumbull once said in one of his speeches, *"Every person and every nation must take lessons in God's school of adversity. 'We can say, "Blessed is night, for it reveals to us the stars." In the same way we can say, "Blessed is sorrow, for it reveals God's comfort." The floods washed away home and mill, all the poor man had in the world. But as he stood on the scene of his loss, after the water had subsided, brokenhearted and discouraged, he saw something shining in the bank which the waters had washed bare. "It looks like gold," he said.* **It was gold. The flood which had beggared him made him rich.** *So it is oftentimes in life"*.

I can attest to this excerpt as through it all, I physically saw the difference in my level of trust and belief in God. I grew richer in my spirit and felt like an innocent child again. I learned that false pride is driven by the ego and humility is directly connected to divinity. It was not difficult for me to conclude that the ego is driven by false pride. I remember from personal experience, in my early 20's when I was employed to work with investors who were known to be amongst the leaders in the hedge fund investment, I was sometimes over-confident and in my naïve state, I would sweat the small simple things that didn't matter. The ego would often grow bigger than my spirit and the reason for this was that my focus was on the position I held. I directly reported to the general partner and I was exposed to privileged and confidential information as well as high-profile individuals. With exposure to such individuals and information, I was slightly conceited and now I can compare the different times and how the challenges were some of the methods God used to prune me when the ego would try to get the best of me.

During the times when I encountered more intense obstacles, I had very little concern for the temporal and focused only on that which was *purpose related*. At this point, the spirit itself was growing in awareness of the potential that was within me. As I experienced the true essence of humanity, I became more conscious of the need for human resources and felt that God's purpose for my being must be fulfilled with a humble approach. It became fun for me to celebrate personal growth and appreciate the pruning as it has widened my views of life.

The main concern I had was to raise my son the way a competent parent is supposed to, and I tried my best to give him all that I had which were the little seeds that will grow into trees of life and produce substantial fruits in due season. Manners, respect for other human beings, responsibility for his actions, community involvement, self-esteem and teachings from effective leaders that brought forth a spiritual connection with him and God were some of the values I instilled in my son. Even though these were not tangible gifts, I believe without a doubt that all these will bring forth the tangible at the appointed time. *[Train up a child in the way he should go and when he is old he will not depart from it - Proverbs 22 vs. 6.]* I learnt this first hand at home and at Sunday school.
In one of his sermons, Archbishop Leighton interpreted the words of the Apostle Paul as follow:

"When the Apostle Paul was on his way to Jerusalem where he foresaw that "bonds and afflictions" awaited him, he could say triumphantly, "BUT NONE OF THESE THINGS MOVE ME." Everything in Paul's life and experience that could be shaken had been shaken, and he no longer counted his life, or any of life's possessions, dear to him. And we, if we will but let God have His way with us, may come to the same place, so that neither the fret and tear of little things of life, nor the great and heavy trials, can have power to move us from the peace that passeth understanding, which is declared to be the portion of those who have learned to rest ONLY on God. "Him that **overcometh** will I make a pillar in the temple of my God; and he shall go no more out."

Self-improvement

Based on the definition of the words *joy* and *valley*, did I truly experience joy while encountering these challenges?

Joy - *the emotion evoked by well-being, success, or good fortune or by the prospect of possessing what one desires.*

Valley – *in geology, a valley also called a vale, dale, glen or strath is a depression with predominant extent in one direction.*

This may seem like a paradox, but, yes, "*joy*" was present during difficult times as I was directly connected with the ***Joy of the Lord***, which is my strength. At this point in the journey, my focus was changed and my emotional reactions were placed under the control of the Spirit of God, I refused to allow anyone or anything to steal my peace. I made a conscious choice to rise above the issues of life that came about by egoistic responses to opposition and adversity.

With a new mind-set, a new attitude towards my purpose was birthed. The best thing I could have done was to leave behind all the things that had brought defilement to my soul and spirit; it doesn't' mean that I have forgotten them as I don't suffer memory loss. I simply chose not to use them as means of retaliating. I began to experience multiplied opportunities to rise to a new level of peace and love, when I realized that if I am to attain my objective, I must establish and maintain valid priorities, beginning with sincere desires and faith.

My faith had been tested and found to be strong because I chose to believe God's words and I believe that this transition was preparing me for my own advancement. When I quieted my soul, watched intently and listened carefully, the cobwebs of confusion and disarray that kept me from operating at maximum efficiency were revealed to me. God has always confirmed his words and being sensitive and yielding to the unction of the Holy Spirit gave me patience to do nothing until I was spiritually moved and had the peace that surpasses my own understanding.

Considering the many challenges I faced and after discovering the truth about the conditions, the joy came about along with the revelation; *revelation brings knowledge* and I no longer had to search for the truth. I knew I had the power to change my condition with the knowledge I gained and being in the know gave me the strength to move forward. Yes, my emotions were involved and while it was attacked by deception, I felt being able to see beyond the obstacles gave me a sense of peace and I realized that my success lie in the true me, which is the spirit. [*It is the Spirit who gives life; the flesh accomplishes nothing. The words that I have spoken to you are spirit and life – John 6:63*].

The valley, state of being, at one point appeared rather depressing and I felt stagnant. When I compared my life before Jacob and the rest of challenges that came after, I was reminded of the good-natured people who I was accustomed to associating myself with and the kindness I exchanged and experienced; it was rather difficult for me to be satisfied with my current condition. On the contrary, I counted my blessings, naming the wisdom that I was gaining, the gift of life and all the good things that sustained me. Ryanne was very supportive and there were several random acts of kindness I exchanged with others that I met along the way that outweighed the conspirators and their games. Where joy came in was that I was aware of my situation and I took a realistic and honest approach in dealing with myself. I was steadfast in seeking the right counsel and associated myself with people who esteemed themselves and human beings with high regards.

Hannah Whitall Smith confirmed my every move and the opposition and adversity that I faced with this excerpt:

"To be as immovable as a pillar in the house of our God, is an end for which one would gladly endure all the shakings that may be necessary to bring us there!

When God is in the midst of a kingdom or city, He makes it as firm as Mount Zion that cannot be removed. When He is in the midst of a soul, though calamities throng about it on all hands, and roar like the billows of the sea, yet there is a constant calm within, such a peace as the world can neither give nor take away. What is it but want of lodging God in the soul and that in

His stead the world is in men's hearts that make them shake like leaves at every blast of danger? Can it be possible that we, who are so easily moved by the things of earth, can arrive at a place where nothing can upset us or disturb our clam? Yes, it is possible; and the apostle Paul knew it."

CHAPTER 7

RECOVERY

My Destiny is Divine; I DO NOT NEED TO SEE ONE FALL FOR ME TO RISE – Sophia Melanie Manning

*"Success is not final, failure is not fatal: it is the **courage to continue that counts**."* Winston Churchill

"I will keep my eyes on the prize". The prize is my **destiny, goals, loved ones**, **true friends, life, health, peace, joy, success** and is **NOT** the haters, talebearers, enemies, foes, traitors, conspirators, nay-sayers, or negative energy.

Knowing that God gave me great and precious promises and even though they were not fulfilled as I assumed, I know that what God had promised will be fulfilled, no matter what; and so, my focus was not on the promises, but on the Almighty Himself. I practiced detaching emotionally and sought wisdom and direction, which is abundantly available from God; good reports, great results and newness began to locate me from all directions. "*To God be the glory*"

"*I will give you a new heart and put a new spirit in you; I will remove from you your heart of stone and give you a heart of flesh. And I will put my Spirit in you and move you to follow my decrees and be careful to keep my laws*" - **Ezekiel 36 verse 26-27**

The time to grow the fruit of a new season had begun and as this tree of life planted by living waters came to fruition, **[RESULTS]**; this acronym came to mind with least effort:

RESOLVE

EVERY

SITUATION;

UNITE IN

LOVE

TOGETHER WE FIND THE

SOLUTION

What better way to tell this story; from discovery to recovery, the wrong decision lead me in the right direction and resulted in my *destination*. I can now better appreciate process and substance as my experience has brought practical results - grow-flow-stay in the know.

The word *"joy"* has several words with similar meanings – *delight, happiness, pleasure, enjoyment, elation, joyfulness, jubilation* and *excitement* to name some. In retrospect, I honestly believe that through times of desolation, all of those words described my emotional state when I experienced situations and conditions that usually find one in a contrary state as I felt peace and freedom in my spirit. It was all in the hands of God, even when I would try to reason the facts I couldn't find a substantial answer.

The one thing I cherished about the valley season is that the "***joy***" I experienced gave me *freedom* and *purpose*. I often think of the many ways to use my experiences for the benefit and betterment of mankind. Even through times of difficulties and unexpected uncontrollable circumstances, I was able to handle myself in a way that no one could have read my countenance accurately and I believe that being at peace in such times, was victory in itself. I remember when my divorce was final and I changed my name, a fellow co-worker asked if I got married and when I said it was the other way around, she said, "you wear it well".

With my story, one of the main things that hit me hard was the loss of the literature that I compiled when my laptop was destroyed, but Ryanne got a custom built personal computer with advanced features. At this time, I was forced to see the brighter side of things, and I indeed made progress as I created new projects that had more substance that will reach a broader audience than originally intended. When I had car issues, someone was kind enough to fund the repair and two years later Ryanne got a car in excellent condition; lots of tangible blessings to count.

When my aunt passed away in another state and a friend that I met in the law firm where I contracted called me; I told her about my aunt's death and I wasn't planning on going to the funeral as the arrangements were rather sudden. Without my asking her for assistance, she initiated kindness by giving me one hundred dollars and introduced me to one of her associates that worked with the airlines who gave me a pass for the trip. Ah! You see! I must keep the positive energy flowing, "*joy in the valley*"

At the same time when untrue tales were being circulated about me, God was using another person to line up a job for me which kept me employed until I was able to produce projects of my own. After two years of employment with the law firm, in the same building, one floor above my office, the medical professionals hired Ryanne to work two summers and he gained experience, money and meaningful relationships.

Later when my job changed insurance provider, to my surprise the dentist who was assigned to my plan was no stranger to my family. She went to dental school with one of my first cousins in another state and when Ryanne became her patient, she encouraged him to consider working with her to gain experience in the field of dentistry to expand his horizons. Ryanne accepted an offer to work with the dental practice before graduating from high school and held the position through the summer and thereafter. Ryanne graduated cum laude of his graduating class and was accepted at a university ranked amongst the top ten universities of the nation. To the single mom or the family that struggles with these challenges, this piece of the testimony is for you; "*keep the faith – **joy is in the valley**.*"

In consciously applying the fruits of the Spirit to situations, I made tremendous progress in my personal character and knew that I was growing. I recall in my immature days, I would not have sought God's direction and would perhaps find it harder to release the people who offended me and perhaps responded in a like way. I have learned that words and deeds are birthed out of emotions that are connected to some spirit that is not necessarily from the known fruits of the Spirit. When the insults, false judgment and misrepresentations came, I was able to face them all with love and thought of it as an opportunity for growth and I grew indeed in actions. I can truly say as Joseph did in Genesis, "*God made me fruitful in the land of my affliction*". – **Genesis 41 v. 52.**

LOVE

OVERCOMES AND IS

VICTORIOUS

EVERY TIME

I took to heart the words of Dr. Jowett who said *"God does not comfort us to make us comfortable, but to make us **comforters**" and was then reminded of these words: "It is in giving you receive, it is in pardoned you are pardon, it is dying to oneself, you gain eternal life"* – St. Francis of Assisi

I hereby extend my highest regard to a very great, but very humble man of God; Dr. Kent M. Keith who wrote *The Paradoxical Commandments* and hereby express my gratitude for his direct authorization in allowing me to reference this legendary vintage piece of writing in my story. Dr. Keith, "*The Paradoxical Commandments*" contributed much *joy to my valley*; I salute you! It is also an honor to know that this was later modified by Mother Teresa from Calcutta, India who entitled it "*The Final Analysis*, she is indeed an example to the human race.

This well-cherished *Paradoxical Commandments* came in very handy during the times of testing.

The Paradoxical Commandments
By Dr. Kent M. Keith

People are illogical, unreasonable, and self-centered. *Love them anyway.*

If you do good, people will accuse you of selfish ulterior motives. *Do good anyway*

If you are successful, you will win false friends and true enemies. *Succeed anyway*

The good you do today will be forgotten tomorrow. *Do good anyway.*

Honesty and frankness make you vulnerable. *Be honest and frank anyway*

The biggest men and women with the biggest ideas can be shot down by the smallest men and women with the smallest minds. *Think big anyway.*

People favor underdogs but follow only top dogs. *Fight for a few underdogs anyway*

What you spend years building may be destroyed overnight. *Build anyway.*

People really need help but may attack you if you do help them. *Help people anyway.*

Give the world the best you have and you'll get kicked in the teeth. *Give the world the best you have anyway.*

IT IS MY VALLEY – I CHOOSE "JOY"

"*In the final analysis, it is all between you and God; it was never between you and them anyway*" – Mother Teresa of Calcutta, India.

It was a TEST and everyone I had encountered, whether verbal or otherwise, were involved, just like a puzzle, every piece had to be applied to make it complete; but it is always between God and the individuals.

The valley season was not about the disappointments, misunderstandings or the treacherous deceptions; it was simply a TEST that was between the Creator and me. I believe He brought me to higher heights in Him – it is not usual for one to be given a test without preparation, unless he is being evaluated on his level of knowledge of a particular subject. It is not valid to test elementary students with high school level exam; or for elementary students to conduct classes with high school scholars, so, the method of testing proved to be a test in itself and I did not by any means disturb it. It was a personal relationship with the creator even though it involved other people and situations; the *antagonist* had to be present. **TRIED ON EVERYSIDE; IT IS A TEST**. I believe this period taught me more than any formal studies that I have attended during my years of higher educational studies.

The main testimony is that I am equipped with the essential tools for life that I can pass down as legacy to people that cross my path through reading this book. I definitely saw the opportunity to live by the words of St. Francis of Assisi in the difficulties that presented themselves and as *Rainer Maria Rike* once said, "perhaps all the dragons of our lives are princesses who are only waiting to see us once beautiful and brave. Perhaps everything terrible is in its deepest being something helpless that wants help from us."

Life goes on, and I must get past the injustices that have brought wounds to my soul. I must focus on the plan and purpose for my life, and if I allow these violations to fester and become bitterness they will stand in the way of my progress. I do not want to get stuck here by rehearsing the events that caused me to suffer. I decided to make a conscious decision to forgive, knowing that this wrongdoing did not have its root or beginning with God, according to Jeremiah – *God's plan is for a future and a hope.* This was a scheme of the enemy to disable me and keep me from fulfilling the Divine purposes, and I decided to resist the united forces of evil and move on. – [the enemy comes to steal, kill and destroy one's divine destiny]

Mark 4:37; *and there arose a great storm.*
"Some of the storms of life come suddenly; a great sorrow, a bitter disappointment, a crushing defeat. Some come slowly. They appear upon the ragged edges of the horizon no larger than a man's hand, but, trouble that seems so insignificant spreads until it covers the sky and overwhelms us. Yet it is in the storm that God equips us for service. When God wants an oak He plants it on the moor where the storms will shake it and

*the rains will beat down upon it, and it is in the midnight battle when elements that the oak wins its rugged fiber and becomes the king of the forest. When God wants to make a man He puts him into some storm. The history of mankind is always rough and rugged. No man is made until he has been out into the surge of the storm and found the sublime fulfillment of the prayer: "O God, take me, break me, make me". Every man who is preeminent for his ability was first preeminent for suffering. The beauties of nature come after the storm. The rugged beauty of the **mountain** is born in a storm, and the heroes of life are the storm-swept and battle-scarred. You have been in the storms and swept by the blasts. Have they left you broken, weary, beaten in the **valley,** or have they lifted you to the sunlit summits of a richer, deeper, more abiding manhood and womanhood? Have they left you with more sympathy with the storm-swept and the battle-scarred?*

God will not only deliver you; but in doing so, you will be given a lesson that you will never forget, and to which, in many psalm and song, in after days, you will revert. You will never be able to thank God enough for having done just as He has." The Storm" painted by Pierre-Auguste Cot, a French artist born in Paris (1837-1883).

Friends, I paid my dues ... **JOY IN THE VALLEY** is my song.

While I will admit that it was not always easy for me to exercise the words that describe the fruits of the Spirit, I will say that through practice, I have become better at my approach in making decisions. I will also admit that I made mistakes along the way in trusting the wrong people and making choices that were not the best, but as I recognized the forces that were against me, I was proactive in withdrawing myself in order to keep the positive energy flowing. I am often reminded that even though people make mistakes, God sees potential, hearts and motives, so I encourage you to look within yourself and find your potential and align it with the right motives so you too can experience joy in your valley. One writer said, *"The person without flaws is the one you don't know well"* – unknown.

This selection taken from a daily devotional clearly explains the fruit of the Spirit, "patience". *"Abraham was long tried, but he was richly rewarded. The Lord tried him by delaying to fulfill His promise. Satan tried him by temptation; men tried him by jealousy, distrust, and opposition; Sarah tried him by her peevishness. But he patiently endured. He did not question God's veracity, nor limit His power, nor doubt His faithfulness, nor grieve His love; but he bowed to divine sovereignty, submitted to infinite wisdom, and was silent under delays, waiting the Lord's time. And so, having patiently endured, he obtained the promise. God's promises cannot fail of their accomplishment. Patient waiters cannot be disappointed. Beloved, Abraham's conduct condemns a hasty spirit, reproves a murmuring one, commends a patient one, and encourages quiet submission to God's will and way. Remember, Abraham was tried; he patiently waited; he received the promise and was satisfied. Imitate his example, and you will share the same blessing. "And so, after he had patiently endured, he obtained the promise"* [Heb. 6:15] Unknown.

I stood in the power of the **Almighty** and my faith and strength were renewed. God Himself brought me through many trials and many fires of adversity and built a reservoir of knowledge and wisdom within me that must be preserved, released and distributed to my fellow brethren who need to know what I have known and experienced. My testimony will encourage others to persevere and trust God to the end because they can see for themselves that I have come through much tribulation in victory.

Faith in God's promises and *belief in myself* became my personal logo. I couldn't help but cherish the acronym [B-E-L-I-E-V-E] spelt out on Darlene Bishop's Television Broadcast; I began to use this as a daily reminder that victory is certain because God lives.

B-E-L-I-E-V-E

BECAUSE

EMANUEL [God with us]

LIVES

I

EXPECT

VICTORY

EVERYTIME

Self-advancement

RESULTS

The results of the valley season were personal development and growth in my spiritual walk, my attitude towards fellow man is more refined and I have a greater appreciation for human and natural resources.

My personal ABC of the valley season resulted in **advancement**; I got **better,** not *bitter* and I **continue** to strive for the best in every area of my life. I was distracted on several occasions, but didn't allow the distractions to bring destruction – DISTRACTION BRINGS DESTRUCTION IF YOU ALLOW IT. There is always room for improvement, admitting my weaknesses and striving for substance has become my mission, *what a joyful journey*? I am changing and evolving for the **better.**

As I grew in maturity and saw that a greater and more effective level of stewardship were entrusted in my care by God Himself, through diligent and responsible management, I was careful not to squander my valuable resources. I increased in wisdom and prospered in several exceptional ways. I had to come to the realization that I am not destined to live under the rules of emotional oppression; I am dedicated to victory and will not succumb to discouragement and defeat.

Fear of failure was not allowed to gain grounds in my heart and life, for I know I am directly connected to the source of life – the '**Creator**". The perplexing and tumultuous times did not diminish my faith, but my faith grew instead. I saw the trying and testing as opportunities to stretch my faith to believe God. I am now better prepared to experience the ups and downs of life and to **OVERCOME!**

The key to my success in the matters I faced was *determination* and I was growing according to *divine specifications.* When I was faced with fierce opposition, I was able to discern the attacks and knew that I was moving towards a new spiritual plateau and this level was not easy to achieve. With tenacity, I set my face strong against opposing forces, was stronger and more courageous in standing this new ground, knowing that God's divine purpose was being manifesting in the earth.

I knew I was entering a time of advancement to break through barriers that range from minor issues to significant and momentous change when I felt a sudden lift from the pressures that weighted me down and I began to experience a sense of release and freedom. I then maximized this time of joy with thanksgiving and praises to God.

I know that my passion and purpose towards fellow human beings is to make a difference of some kind, thus, I will continue to pursue my dreams regardless of the consequences. The folks that did me wrong and tried to build a negative reputation of me didn't gain anything substantial. I believe in due season the laws of nature and creation will have the final words as mentioned in the Holy Scriptures – "*sowing and reaping*".

I am by nature jovial, I enjoy meeting people from different levels of life and background and exchanging ideas; in doing so, I know that people of all temperament, stages and kind are going to be in the crowd. The words of Jesus of Nazareth teaches, "*Let both grow together until the harvest: and in the time of harvest I will say to the reapers, Gather ye together first the tares, and bind them in bundles to burn them: but gather the wheat into my barn.* **Matt. 13 verse 30.** Perhaps if I were in their shoes, I would have been tempted to act the way they did. Their actions have taught me consequences indirectly that I wouldn't want to have to bear, so in seeing the glass half-full, they were all teachers of some sort as I learned from some of their mistakes.

I echo the following words from Og Mandino and would like you to personalize it as well to get the best life has to offer, *"I am nature's greatest miracle. I am not on this earth by chance. I am here for a purpose and that purpose is to **grow into a mountain**, not to shrink to a grain of sand. Henceforth will I apply all my efforts to become the highest mountain of all and I will strain my potential until it cries for mercy. I will increase my knowledge of mankind, myself and purpose, thus my seed will multiply. I will practice, and improve, and polish the words I utter **to articulate my thoughts**, for this is the foundation on which I will build my life. Also will I seek constantly to improve my manners and graces,* *for they are the sugar to which all are attracted." —* ["articulate my thoughts" modified to suit my story]

I had to change the lens in which I viewed situations, I adjusted and adapted to the unfamiliar as deemed necessary, but became wiser in my decisions as I faced the facts. I learned firsthand that storms exist to slow me down, not to stop me. The word *endurance* had a new meaning to me as I lived through times when all seemed to have failed, but continued existence was my focus; after all, I had life and all the necessities and was determined to make the best of it all. I made major improvements in every area of my life as I see where the four basic elements of mathematics were played out in my journey. God had to **subtract** all the waste and contaminated energy, **divide** my strengths in order for me to be balanced, thus much were **added** and then **multiplied**.

"**Fail your way forward.** Recognize that *ready, fire, aim* is superior to r*eady, aim, aim, aim. Straightforward trial and error produces better results than endless vacillating. If you're afraid to make decisions and act on them in the face of ambiguity and uncertainty, get a job. Failure's lessons are essential to success."* Steve Pavlina

MY PRAYER ANSWERED
LORD MAKE ME AN INSTRUMENT OF THY PEACE

Where there is hatred, let me sow love; - This prayer is not just a set of easy words to ask, but is rather challenging. When I was faced with deception, violent ill-will, verbal abuse and constant oppression through unseen actions and subtle deeds, I chose to send silent blessings in love and kept smiling at the storm.

Where there is injury, pardon; - Countless injustice came my way, "*instant forgiveness*" were the words written on my heart and I practiced continued efforts to improve my attitude towards the assigned agents.

Where there is doubt, faith; - There were those who doubted me because of their own preconceived stereotypes and limited views on life; in the long run after it all played itself out and time revealed the truth, they all changed their minds and I changed mine as well.

Where there is despair, hope; - When it seemed as if there was no confidence or hope, I encouraged myself, embraced the present and receive it as a gift from the Creator.

Where there is darkness, light; - At times when light was absent and I experienced total gloom on personal and distant levels, I chose to mentally light a candle instead of cursing the darkness by *appreciating* the reason for light which is to dispel darkness.

Where there is sadness; joy – My spirit was often attacked with the situations I faced, I had to be strong and the joy of the Lord became my strength; it was easy to share joy as it came natural from within.

O divine Master, grant that I may not so much seek – In my experience in the various areas of life, I have found that there is always room for improvement. When I discovered that the environment really needed positive energy, I thought that I should be proactive in extending that which I have rather than looking for someone to fulfill God's Divine duty – *"kindness acts like a boomerang, give it; get it back".*

To be consoled as to console; - As I journeyed along, I would often get encouraging feed-back from people that would often tell me that I have raised their spirit with my positive attitude. Yes! I love to console; it requires a self-less heart.

To be understood as to understand; - I was certain that my motives were right and so, my priority was not so much that my "*non-generic*" customs were understood, but that I understood the situations and the reasons for such behaviors. For example, limited people would tend to send limitations to others. Folks with low self-esteem found it pleasurable to subdue others, the insecurities seemed related to insincerity and overall lack of knowledge is just like being blind. It was important for me to understand that, so I could maintain a clear conscience.

To be loved as to love; - In loving the unlovable, I became better and chose to even want to become better and even better. I saw the need to want to become better, not to accomplish more; unless the more is a result of the better. – *It never fails* – LOVE THEM ANYWAY!

For it is in giving that we receive; - It is my pleasure to quote one of my favorite all time ancient writers, Kahil Gibran, *"you give but little when you give of your possessions. It is when you give of yourself that you truly give."*

It is in pardoning that we are pardoned; - Another favorite writer who I dearly admire, Dale Carnegie puts it this way, *"any fool can criticize, condemn and complain, but it takes character and self-control to be understanding and **forgiving**.* The critics came from all directions, but I was not moved as it was all due to the limitations and ignorance of the sources; but again, that was an opportunity to sow the seed of pardon as us mankind will also need to be pardoned.

It is in dying to self that we are born to eternal life – Dying to self was not an easy task, but was more like a transformation that kept me consciously evolving; it was a rather interesting journey with God's grace. I would much rather hear the words "she lived a great life" than "her physical features were appealing". I would rather live an enriched life of fulfillment than to live a long life only to fill it with self-absorption, body maintenance, and image repair. I am glad that divinity brought me to discover the prayer of *St. Francis of Assisi* and while he has not been around for centuries, I will say that this prayer was of great substance to me as I experienced *"Joy In The Valley"*.

SUMMARY AND CONCLUSION

"Painting what I experience, translating what I feel is like a great liberation. But it is also work, self-examination, consciousness, criticism, struggle." **Balthus**

Albert Einstein once said, *"I want to know God's thoughts; the rest are details."* In recognizing myself beyond ignorance, I used the experiences and exposures that I gained throughout my life to design a new path for my goals. I set short and long-term goals, mapped out different routes to achieve each mark and ensure myself that I am an *instrument of fulfillment*, and whatever goals I set would benefit mankind.

The valley gave me the opportunity to redeem the times of disappointment, heartache, hardships, loss of vitality and loss of prosperity. I was able to reinstate the full rights of God's promises. Obedience to God, belief in His faithfulness brought me a long way and has led me into the goodness that He prepared me for. In forgetting that which is behind and realizing the obstacles as distraction and hindrance, I saw myself at a higher place where God imparted more wisdom and revelation as I was not bound to the former things, former disappointments and heartaches.

The seed of God's kingdom is within me and it was up to me to allow it to manifest, grow, and mature. The valley season was indeed a stepping stone to complete freedom; it would be worth nothing to me if

I was able to see all truth theoretically instead of experientially and the door for my continued progression and freedom is wide open.

In order for me to discern and perceived the hindering forces that created confusion and misunderstanding, I had to be still and that was when the perverse spirit sent to keep me from accomplishing my goals and purposes by undermining my confidence was revealed. Those barriers were indeed broken when I placed my faith and trust in God alone. I can boldly say that God has led me into a broad place where there are no restraints; "**Joy in the Valley is an eternal song.**"

I practiced the process of filling my mind with love, gratitude and forgiveness. I became proactive and searched for hobbies that are fulfilling, sent silent blessings and refuse to be seduced into joining any network of contaminated low energy. At times I would often think of the present positive happenings in my life: Ryanne and I have everything we need, sanity, health, nature is always kind to us, the weather is good; the mean-spirited people are giving me the opportunity to sow love in the midst of hatred, pardon where there is deliberate injury, I know in the long-run, the doubtful will change to believing; simply put, the journey is the reward. Words without *proven* actions never stand firm; I believe when an action is completed with a sense of purpose, it never fails; I found that I had to stick to the words of St. Francis' prayer.

I faced challenges and obstacles with a realistic view; I got a reality check in the valley, thus, persistently abstaining from falsehood. When the negative forces came against me, I would often think of thoughts that are fruitful and harmless. I absolutely love music and would often dance and sing along with my favorite songs to ease my mind from chaos and confusion. As Moses used his rod to lead his followers to the promise land, so I used music to lead myself out of the valley to the destination of my benchmark.

One interesting observation I discovered was that people would constantly accuse me of their opinions out of ignorance or because they were surface-based, I later found out that I was judged on their familiar standards and surroundings. At this point, I had the opportunity to be independent of the accusations of others and purposed myself to be immune to anger and hurt over what others accuse me of. I am kind and jovial because that is the way I am, not because of the reactions I want from others or because I am seeking any external reward.

I believe that kindness that is backed by sincerity will suffice to keep me from being subdued and infected by false accusation. In conjunction to connecting to the Divine through prayers, and other excerpts mentioned in this book, the most significant methods I used to succeed and overcome were **forgiveness, love and productivity**. I was spiritually sensitive and listened for God's direction; I was flexible to take advantage of unexpected opportunities that ultimately brought all the circumstances and challenges into divine order.

The invisible spiritual essence of me is expressed by my actions for the benefit and betterment of my fellow human being that adds to my personal fulfillment, and so, my focus is on what I know to be my *divine purpose*. I did not know the basis of my accusers, so I did not defend myself, I saw the need to be in a **state of grace.** The one thing I know that I **mastered** was to deviate from occasions to be offended, judged or labeled others, as I believe that when one is in a **state of grace**, he is connected to God and is free from the effects of those external forces.

Overall, total surrender to God was the solitary way that brought me deep convictions and consolation. If it were not for the challenges and obstacles that I faced, I don't think I would have known the real meaning of the fruit *joy* and learn how to connect it to the Spirit. *"It was good for me to be afflicted so that I might learn your decrees"*; Psalm 119 verse 71.

From the grassroots, I encourage you to bear fruits even in times of desolation. Fertile ground is that which is bare; cultivate fruits of greatness in the open ditches as the Holy Scriptures suggests, 2 Kings Chapter 3 verses 16 -17, *"Thus saith the Lord, Make this valley full of ditches. For thus saith the Lord, Ye shall not see wind, neither shall ye see rain; yet that valley shall be filled with water, that ye may drink, both ye, and your cattle, and your beasts."* The valley season will expire in due season;

"ALL THINGS ARE POSSIBLE TO THOSE WHO BELIEVE."

To my beloved fellow mankind I implore you to refuse to allow situations that will require compromise, apathy, and even apostasy to weaken your faith and undermine your foundation. Ignore the need for approval or fear of rejection; take "**no**" as a legitimate answer. Without hesitation, stand only on the rock of your faith in God; the Creator is also the one who breathes in you, is with you always and will give you the courage to withstand it all. Again, THE ANSWER IS "**ALL OF THE ABOVE**".

I will conclude with the following words from the Legendary Dr. Charles Stanley: *"Suffering is unavoidable. It comes without warning; it takes us by surprise. It can shatter or strengthen us. It can be the source of great bitterness or abounding joy. It can be the means by which our faith is destroyed. Or it can be the tool through which our faith is deepened. The outcome hinges not on the nature or source of our adversity, but on the character and spirit of our response. Our response to adversity will for the most part be determined by our reason for living, our purpose for being on this earth, as we see it."*

Words from the Holy Scriptures: *"after you have suffered for a little while, the God of all grace, who called **you** to His eternal glory in Christ, **will Himself perfect, confirm, strengthen and establish you"**.* – 1 Peter 5 vs. 10.

With love, ***"JOY" IN THE VALLEY IS MY SONG***
– Sophia Melanie Manning

FROM THE VALLEY; "I INSPIRE YOU"

"My destiny is Divine; I DO NOT NEED TO SEE ONE FALL FOR ME TO RISE" – *Sophia Manning*

"A challenge could be an indication that you are on the right path" - *Sophia Manning*

"To dream anything that you want to dream, that is the beauty of the human mind. To do anything that you want to do, that is the strength of the human will. To trust yourself to test your limits, that is the courage to succeed." – *Bernard Edmonds*

"You have enemies? Good. That means you've stood up for something, sometime in your life." – *Winston Churchill*

"Commit yourself to a dream ... Nobody who tried to do something great but fails is a total failure. *Why*? Because he can always rest assured that he succeeded in life's most important battle – he defeated the fear of trying" – *Robert H. Schuller*

"Our Similarities bring us to a common ground; Our Differences allow us to be fascinated by each other" – *Tom Robbins*

"We the willing, led by the unknowing, are doing the impossible for the ungrateful. We have done so much, with so little, for so long, we are now qualified to do anything, with nothing." – *Mother Teresa*

"The world is not in need of a new religion, nor is the world in need of a new philosophy; what the world needs is healing and regeneration. The world needs people who, through devotion to God, are so filled with the spirit that they can be *instruments* through which healing take place, because healing is important to everybody." *Joel S. Goldsmith*

"In matter of the spirit, it is never the number, but the strength of the ideas that conquers" - *a great Impressionist 1800's*

Biography

Sophia Melanie Manning, founder and CEO of Entertainment Now Network, Inc., an all-inclusive entertainment organization that embraces all aspects of the arts; her mission is to enhance the entertainment industry by consciously creating situations to actualize her potential. She is also the founder, executive director, and international correspondent for Children Are First Network, a non-profit organization dedicated to helping under-privilege children globally.

Sophia is currently pursuing her doctorate of Arts and Letters, holds a Masters in Liberal Arts, has completed semesters of studies in Masters of Public Administration, a Bachelor of Science degree in Business Administration, and is a professional paralegal with a certificate from an American Bar Association Paralegal Institution.

Sophia is the author of "Joy In The Valley, she writes, directs and produces 'For Children's Sake" that showcases the best in children. She is a creative writer determined to adding value to the entertainment industry and uses every spear moment to meditate on consciousness and reality. She writes quality projects that have substance, promotes laughter, restoration, and is safe for a wide-audience. As reflected in her writings, she envisions the entire universe benefiting from intriguing stories, conscious lyrics, and literature. She believes in living and sharing life to its fullest, and that when we unite the forces *love, harmony and joy*, we create success and good fortune with effortless ease.

With her positive attitude, her intriguing testimony reflects the *true purpose* for her valley season which brought forth fruits such as Children Are First Network, For Children's Sake, Inspire You, Soul Saving Party, The Joy Valley Collection, Joy-In-The-Valley, and several other projects. **Sophia** has been victorious over many obstacles and challenges and has concluded that the creator of the universe is the sole source of life, restoration and healing. By applying love, joy, peace, and **forgiveness** to challenging situations, pruning periods and valley-season believes "*life is worth living when you know how to live*". She enjoys serving children, listening to conscious music, writing and traveling.

The author will donate fifty percent [50%] of the income from the sale of this book to non-profit organizations that support underprivileged children across the world. www.childrenarefirstnetwork.com.

LIFE
Live
It with Love to the
Fullest
Every time …
*****

LOVE
OVERCOMES AND IS
VICTORIOUS
EVERY TIME
*****

LIFE…
WHAT YOU MAKE IT
WHAT YOU ASK
WHAT YOU TELL
WHAT YOU GIVE
WHAT YOU SEEK
WHAT YOU INHABIT

LIFE IS **<u>WORTH</u>** LIVING, WHEN YOU **<u>KNOW</u>**
HOW TO **"LIVE"**

Sophia Melanie Manning

www.ingramcontent.com/pod-product-compliance
Lightning Source LLC
Chambersburg PA
CBHW051805040426
42446CB00007B/524